DETERMINING NEEDS AND APPROPRIATE COUNSELING APPROACHES FOR MEXICAN-AMERICAN WOMEN: A COMPARISON OF THERAPEUTIC LISTENING AND BEHAVIORAL REHEARSAL

BY: TERESA RAMIREZ BOULETTE

San Francisco, California
1976

Published in 1976 by

R AND E RESEARCH ASSOCIATES

4843 Mission St., San Francisco 94112

18581 McFarland Ave., Saratoga, Ca. 95070

Publishers and Distributors of Ethnic Studies

Adam S. Eterovich

Robert D. Reed

Library of Congress Card Catalog Number

75-36572

ISBN

0-88247-374-3

Dr. Boulette is currently employed as Psychologist Coordinator of Outreach Services at Santa Barbara County Mental Health Services, 1216 State St., Santa Barbara, California (1-805-966-2274)

This study was supported by a Ford Foundation Grant in ethnic studies number 710-0224

ACKNOWLEDGMENTS

For the guidance and assistance given me throughout the preparation of this study, I wish to express my appreciation to my dissertation committee, especially to its chairman, Professor Ray Hosford.

Also, I wish to express my gratitude to Thomas Henchy, Ph.D., for his willing and competent assistance.

To the bilingual staff of this study, Ana Alvarez, Maria Inez Martinez, Rita Solinas, Amparo Rios, and Mary Lou Olivos, I would like to express my heartfelt appreciation.

Appreciation is also extended to Hector Alvarez, Phyllis Hosford, Richard Gonzales, Johnnie Roberts, R. N., Esther Ybarra, Colomiro Camacho, Evelyn Ludington, and to the many others who gave me encouragement and much assistance.

Special indebtedness is acknowledged to the Ford Foundation for the financial assistance received from a research grant.

A special thank you is given to my husband, Richard R. Boulette, for his patient and steadfast encouragement throughout the difficult period of this study.

TABLE OF CONTENTS

LIST OF TABLES

CHAPTER I

INTRODUCTION AND REVIEW OF THE LITERATURE

The Mexican American

To understand the needs of Mexican American women for psychological assistance, it is first necessary to gain an understanding
of the psycho-social aspects of this population as a whole. The
Mexican American[1] is this nation's second largest disadvantaged
minority (Table 1). In 1960 their total number of 3,842,000 made
up 2.3 percent of the United States population, 12 percent of
the population of the Southwestern States and 9.1 percent of
California's total population (Barrett, 1966; Grebler et al., 1970).
The 1970 census figures reported by UPI (March 1, 1971) indicates
that 9.2 million persons identify themselves as being Spanish
speaking. Of this number, 5 million are said to be Mexican descent
while 1.4 million are Puerto Rican; 565,000 Cuban; 556,000 Central
and South American; and 1.5 million of other Spanish origin. In
1970, the Mexican American constituted 15.5 percent of California's
total population, a 6.4 percent increase from 1960. (Bureau of
Biostatistics, 1972).

This population is primarily concentrated in Texas, California,
New Mexico, Colorado and Arizona. In 1960, 82 percent of the total
Mexican American population lived in Texas or California, 41.2 per-
cent in California alone (Table 2).

The Mexican American is showing a very rapid population increase. Alisky (1967) estimates that by 1975 the Spanish surnamed
population may well total twenty million. This growth is attributed
in part to their relative youth. In 1960, the median age for the
Mexican American of the Southwest was 20 years, while it was 30
years for the Anglo,[2] and 24 years for the Nonwhite[3] (Grebler et
al., 1970; Barrett, 1966; Moore with Cuellar, 1970). More than
40 percent of the Mexican American Population are children of 15

1

TABLE 1*

Size of Selected Disadvantaged Minority Groups
in the United States - 1960

Negroes	18,900,000
Mexican Americans	3,842,000
Puerto Ricans	983,000
American Indians	524,000
Japanese	464,000
Chinese	237,000
Filipinos	200,000

                                  5   10   15   20

                              Millions of Persons

*Grebler et al., 1970, p. 14.

TABLE 2*

Percentage of Total Southwestern Spanish-Speaking
Population in Each State, 1950 and 1960

	Texas	New Mexico	Colo- rado	Calif- ornia	Ari- zona	Total
% of total Spanish 1950	45.0	10.9	5.2	33.2	5.6	99.9
% of total Spanish 1960	40.9	7.8	4.5	41.2	5.6	100.0

*Barrett, 1966, p. 60, Table 1B.

years or less, while only 30 percent of the Anglo population are in this category (Moore with Cuellar, 1970). State by state comparisons indicate that in California this population is consistently older (Table 3).

A second contributory factor in their population increase is the "... extraordinary fertility of Spanish-surname women (Grebler et al., 1970, p. 13)." Only Afro-Americans in some parts of the South, and rural American Indians match the fertility of the Mexican Americans (Table 4). Moore with Cuellar (1970) state "The young Mexican American women are 41 percent more fertile than Anglos of the same age, and by ages 45-49 (when most Anglo women stop having children) Mexican American women are 107 percent more fertile (p. 57)." Fertility rates for this population average "... 250 more children per 1000 women 15 to 44 years of age than comparable Anglo women--that is, 50 percent higher fertility (Barrett, 1966, p. 177)."

The Mexican American family is not only stressed by having a disproportionately large number of children, but by the absence of the father as well. In 1960, 40 to 50 percent of their families were in the category of "broken homes," i.e., the absence of the father. This phenomenon has rural to urban differences. Farm Mexican American families were more likely to be structurally incomplete than urban families. Barrett (1966) notes "Only one-fourth of all Spanish-speaking rural farm families in the five states have 'Spouse present;' (p. 173)." This high rate of family disruption has also been noted by Grebler et al.,)1970) and Moore with Cuellar (1970).

This population is also disadvantaged by the achievement of consistently low levels of education (Table 5). Education attainment is defined as the number of school years attended. In 1960, the Mexican American, aged 14 and over, averaged four years less schooling than the Anglo and one and a half years less than the Nonwhite. State by state comparisons for 1950 and 1960 (Tables 6 and 7) reveal some educational gain as well as continued marked

3

TABLE 3*

Median Ages of Total White, Spanish-Speaking and Nonwhite Populations, 1950 and 1960

Population	Texas 1950	1960	New Mexico 1950	1960	Colorado 1950	1960	California 1950	1960	Arizona 1950	1960
Total White	28.1	27.4	24.4	23.4	29.6	28.0	32.3	30.3	27.8	26.7
Spanish	19.6	18.0	19.2	18.3	18.2	18.1	22.7	22.1	19.8	19.3
Nonwhite	26.7	24.1	19.3	17.6	28.8	24.8	29.0	25.9	20.3	18.5

*Barrett, 1966, p. 60, Table 6A.

TABLE 4*

Average Number of Persons in the Family, Southwest, 1960

```
        All Families                      Husband-Wife Families,
                                          Family Head Age 35 to 44

6-                                   6-
                                                      5.71
5-                                   5-                          4.74
          4.77                                 4.27
                 4.54
4-                                   4-
     3.39
3-                                   3-

2-                                   2-

1-                                   1-
     Anglo    SS    NW                    Anglo    SS    NW
```

SS - Spanish Surname

NW - Nonwhite

*Grebler et al., 1970, p. 17, Fig. 2-2.

4

TABLE 5*

The Schooling Gap, Southwest, 1960

Median School Years Completed by Persons	Anglo	Spanish Surname	Non - White
14 years and over	12.0	8.1	9.7
14-24	11.3	9.2	10.6
25 and over	12.1	7.1	9.0
Difference from Anglo Schooling, Years			
Age 14 and over	--	3.9	2.3
Age 14-24	--	2.1	0.7
Age 25 and over	--	5.0	3.1
Years of Schooling Completed by Persons 14 Years and Over			
0-4	3.7%	27.6%	15.1%
5-8	22.1	33.8	29.8
9-11	24.3	20.1	24.7
12	27.8	12.8	18.7
Some college	22.1	5.6	11.7

*Grebler et al., 1970, p. 18, Table 2-2.

educational lag and sharp state by state variations. This population's incidence of functional illiteracy (grades 0-4) for males 14 years and over, is very high, 28.6 percent. State by state this breaks down as follows: 30 percent illiteracy for Arizona, 21 percent for California, 17.6 percent for Colorado, 22 percent for New Mexico and 40 percent for Texas (Barrett, 1966). Again Texas and California show great variation, with Texas consistently reporting lower levels of attainment. Overall, the Mexican American's functional illiteracy was seven times higher than that of the Anglo and one and a half higher than that of the Nonwhite (Grebler et al., 1970). Only 13 percent had finished four years of high school and only 5.6 percent had some college education (Grebler et al., 1970). Barrett (1966) additionally points out that in 1960 about 118,000 Mexican Americans had absolutely no

5

TABLE 6*

Median School Years Completed by Spanish-Speaking, Total
White, and Nonwhite Populations, 1950 and 1960**

	Texas 1950	Texas 1960	New Mexico 1950	New Mexico 1960	Colorado 1950	Colorado 1960
Spanish	3.6	6.1	7.4	8.4	6.4	8.6
Total White	9.7	10.8	9.5	11.5	10.9	12.1
Nonwhite	7.0	8.1	5.8	7.1	9.8	11.2

	California 1950	California 1960	Arizona 1950	Arizona 1960
Spanish	7.6	9.0	6.1	7.9
Total White	11.8	12.1	10.6	11.7
Nonwhite	8.9	10.5	5.5	7.0

*Barrett, 1966, p. 179, Table 9A.
**For both sexes, 14 years and over.

formal schooling and about 75 percent of these lived in urban areas.
Even though their educational profile shows some gain between 1950
and 1960, it remains very poor.

This group's economic attainment is also very poor (c.f.
Mittlebach and Marshall, 1966). Their overall economic profile
is very deviant from the Anglo (Table 8). Their family median
annual income for 1959 was 65 percent of the Anglo's income.
Family median annual income is not as reliable an indicator of
poverty as the median annual income per person which takes into
account the Mexican American's consistently larger families. In
1960, their per person median income was 74 percent of the Anglo's
income while the Nonwhite's was 51 percent of the Anglo's income
(Grebler et al., 1970). Thus, this population's annual median
income per person was less than half of the Anglo's and lower than
that of the Nonwhite. Only in Arizona, where the Nonwhite figure
includes many impoverished Indians, is the Nonwhite figure lower
than that of the Mexican American (Table 9). There is a very high
incidence of poverty among Mexican Americans. Defining poverty as

TABLE 7*

School Years Completed by Spanish Speaking Males
14 Years and Over, 1950 and 1960

	Texas		New Mexico		Colorado	
	1950	1960	1950	1960	1950	1960
No. School Years	19.9%	16.0%	8.6%	6.6%	6.9%	5.3%
1-4 Years	33.0	23.5	22.1	15.3	19.5	12.3
5-7 Years	23.2	25.3	26.4	22.5	27.8	22.3
8 years	6.0	9.5	14.0	15.1	17.1	19.2

	California		Arizona	
	1950	1960	1950	1960
	8.4%	8.3%	9.7%	11.5%
	15.4	12.8	20.7	18.6
	20.2	16.2	26.5	21.5
	14.7	14.2	15.5	16.1

High School	(Texas)		(New Mexico)		(Colorado)	
1-3 Years	8.4	13.6	14.2	21.6	15.1	22.9
4 Years	4.0	7.4	7.3	11.8	6.4	11.8
College or More	2.2	4.6	4.1	7.1	2.7	6.1

	(California)		(Arizona)	
	21.2	24.8	13.8	17.5
	11.7	14.9	6.5	9.7
	4.6	8.8	3.2	4.8

*Table 9B, Barrett, 1966, p. 181.

TABLE 8*

The Economic Gap, 1960

Item	Anglo	Spanish Surname	Non-White
Index number (Anglo = 100)			
Median Family Income			
Southwest	100	65	56
Urban Southwest	100	66	59
Median Income per Person in Family			
Southwest	100	47	51
Median Income of Males			
Southwest	100	57	51
Urban Southwest	100	61	53
Median Income Adjusted for Schooling			
Males in California	100	88	72
Males in Texas	100	72	56
Labor Force Participation Rate, Urban, Percent			
Males in Southwest	80.0%	78.0%	78.0%
Females in Southwest	36.0	31.0	46.0
Unemployment Rate, urban, percent			
Males in Southwest	4.5	8.5	9.1
Females in Southwest	5.0	9.5	8.1
Occupational Structure of Males, Urban Southwest			
Percent White Collar	47.0	19.0	18.0
Percent Low-skill Manual	26.0	57.0	60.0
Overall Occupation Position			
(Index: Anglo = 100)	100	84	82
Housing Condition in Metropolitan Areas			
Percent Overcrowded Units	8%	35%	22%
Percent Substandard Units	7	30	27

*Grebler et al., 1970, p. 19, Table 2-3.

TABLE 9*

Median Income per Person in the Family, Spanish-Surname Families
Compared with Other Families, Five Southwest States, 1959

State and Population Group	Income Per Person	Percent of Anglo
Southwest		
Anglo	$2,047	100.0
Spanish-surname	968	47.3
Nonwhite	1,044	51.0
Arizona		
Anglo	1,880	100.0
Spanish-surname	917	48.8
Nonwhites	561	29.8
California		
Anglo	2,255	100.0
Spanish-surname	1,380	61.2
Nonwhite	1,487	63.7
Colorado		
Anglo	1,854	100.0
Spanish-surname	915	49.4
Nonwhite	1,317	71.0
New Mexico		
Anglo	1,828	100.0
Spanish-surname	882	48.3
Nonwhite	557	30.5
Texas		
Anglo	1,772	100.0
Spanish-surname	629	35.5
Nonwhite	755	42.6

*Grebler et al., 1970, p. 185, Table 8-3.

$3,000 or less in annual family income, in 1960, 35 percent of their families were poor. At the same time, less than 16 percent of the Anglos and almost 42 percent of the Nonwhites were in this poverty category (Grebler et al., 1970; Moore with Cuellar, 1970).

Since poor educational attainment and age are some of the factors which influence income, their relationship should be examined. Grebler et al., (1970) compared a homogeneous group of Anglo males with Mexican Americans and Nonwhites of the same age and educational attainment. They found that adjustment for these two variables did not entirely account for the differences in income. A sizeable residual income gap remained which had state by state variation of: six percent for Arizona, 12 percent for California, and 28 percent for Texas (Grebler et al., 1970).
In other words, male Mexican Americans of the same age and education made six percent, 12 percent and 28 percent less than the comparable Anglo sample. This residual income gap occurred for the nonwhite as well as for the Mexican American at all levels of school attainment. Evidence that higher educational attainment does not bring equal financial reward to the Mexican American could be one of the factors which discourage pursuit of more education.

Ethnicity and poor education are only some of the characteristics associated with poverty. The majority (83 percent) of the Mexican American poor families had one or more of the following six characteristics: employment of the family head in farm work; aged family head (65 years and over); broken family (female head of family); under-employment and unemployment; family headed by person under 25 years; and functional illiteracy of family head. In addition, the majority (72 percent) were found to be city dwellers (Grebler et al., 1970).

Nativity and its relation to poverty should be considered. Even though 85 percent of the Mexican Americans of the Southwest are native born, United States nativity seems to be related to higher educational and economic attainment (Barrett, 1966; Moore

10

with Cuellar, 1970). The percentage of native born has increased in each of the five Southwestern states surveyed (Table 10).

The poverty of the Mexican American is influenced by his very high rates of unemployment. Barrett (1966) states:

> In almost all of the states the Spanish-speaking rate of unemployment would be defined as a serious economic crisis if it were characteristic of the total community (p. 188).

Their unemployment rates, which have decreased between 1950 and 1960, remain very high. The 1960 unemployment rate among urban Mexican Americans 14 years and over was 8.5 percent, for the Anglo it was 4.5 percent, and for the Nonwhite 9.1 percent. Thus, this population's rate of unemployment was twice that of the Anglo rate (Table 11). In addition to high unemployment rates, this population also has high under-employment. In California, for example, only 58 percent of urban Mexican American family heads worked 50 to 52 weeks in 1959. This group is further disadvantaged by occupying generally poorer occupational categories (Table 12). When they are compared with Anglos in the same occupational category, Mexican Americans earn less than Anglos. Apparently, this group has the poorer paying jobs within each of the occupational categories. When Mexican Americans are compared to Anglos holding similar jobs, the Mexican American is again found to earn less. Apparently, this group is hired by firms and industries who provide unsteady employment and lower wages. High paying industries may be able to discriminate against this population by enforcing unionization and high educational requirements which may not be relevant to the occupation. Unions are said to discriminate against minorities by refusing to select them for apprenticeships and by failing to admit them even when they possess journeyman skills. Records indicate discrimination against the Mexican Americans by the boiler-makers, machinists and railway carmen unions (Grebler, et al, 1970).

The Mexican American is further disadvantaged by consistently occupying substandard housing: they "... get poorer housing than

11

TABLE 10*

Nativity and Parentage of Spanish-Speaking
1950 and 1960

Nativity and Parentage	Texas		New Mexico		Colorado	
	1950	1960	1950	1960	1950	1960
Native-born	81.8	86.0	95.7	96.1	95.8	96.5
Of native parents	46.5	54.8	87.2	87.4	83.2	86.1
Of foreign or mixed	35.3	31.2	8.5	8.6	12.6	10.4
Of Mexican parents		30.2		8.0		8.5
Other, not reported		1.0		0.6		1.9
Foreign-born	18.2	14.0	4.2	3.9	4.2	3.5
Born in Mexico	17.9	13.6	3.6	3.8	3.7	2.9
Other, not reported	.03	0.4	0.6	0.1	0.5	0.6

*Barrett, 1966, p. 168, Table 4.

TABLE 11*

Percentage of Spanish-surnamed Unemployment
1950 and 1960

		Texas	New Mexico	Colo.	Calif.	Ariz.
Males 14 Years and Over	1950	9.5	11.0	15.6	13.0	13.4
	1960	8.2	10.3	9.5	7.7	6.2

*Barrett, 1966, p. 189.

TABLE 12*

Occupational Distribution of Spanish-surname Males Compared with Other Males, Southwest, 1960

Occupational Category	Urban and Rural			Urban		
	Anglo	Spanish-Surname	Nonwhite	Anglo	Spanish-surname	Nonwhite
Professional	13.7%	3.9%	5.5%	15.1%	4.6%	6.1%
Managers and proprietors	13.8	4.3	3.3	14.7	4.9	3.6
Clerical	7.0	4.6	5.3	7.8	5.5	6.1
Sales	8.3	3.4	2.1	9.2	4.1	2.3
Craftsmen	21.0	15.8	10.1	21.5	18.2	10.8
Operatives	15.9	22.9	19.3	15.8	25.4	20.0
Private household	0.1	0.1	0.8	0.1	0.1	0.9
Service, excluding private household	5.0	7.2	16.6	5.4	8.4	18.6
Laborers	4.7	14.4	18.5	4.4	15.8	18.3
Farm Laborers	2.1	16.0	6.3	0.6	7.3	2.1
Farm managers	3.9	2.2	3.7	0.7	0.6	1.9
Occupation not reported	4.5	5.1	8.7	4.7	5.1	9.3

*Grebler et al., 1970, p. 209, Table 9-2.

do others paying comparable rents (Grebler et al., 1970, p. 262)."
They also have a higher rate of overcrowdedness than do Nonwhites
and a four times higher rate than Anglos. In Texas 47 percent of
the metropolitan Mexican American households were overcrowded
while in California only 27 percent were overcrowded (Grebler et
al., 1970). This population more often not only lives in overcrowded housing units, but their homes are more likely to be
delapidated than are those of Anglos. In the Southwest nearly
30 percent of all housing units, according to Grebler (Grebler et
al., 1970), occupied by Mexican Americans were delapidated,
compared to 7.5 percent for Nonwhites. Of the units occupied by
this population, 13.1 percent were without baths as compared to
4.4 of the Anglo homes. The rate of housing delapidation for
the Mexican Americans showed no decline since 1950 even though
the rate of overcrowdedness improved. Associated with poor housing
are other deprivations such as substandard playgrounds; inadequate street lights; neglected street and sidewalk pavement; substandard schools; inadequate transportation and shopping facilities; exposure to drug use, stealing and police harassment; ex-
ploitation; and the depressing milieu of poverty.

Needed Psychological Services

The demographic profile of the Mexican American documents
their disadvantaged position and provides support for their urgent
need for psychological services as well. The relationship between
low socio-economic status and mental disorders is a very compli-
cated one. The vague, contradictory and often unmeasurable criteria
for mental health and illness (Sells, 1965; Clausen, 1968; Gardner,
1968); the different case finding methods; the lack of a definite
continuum between social class and mental illness; and the great
heterogeneity of the culture of poverty (Will and Vatler, 1965;
Clerk, 1964; Clinard, 1970) contribute to the complexity of this
relationship. Nevertheless, there is much evidence that supports
the belief that the lowest socio-economic class have by far the
greatest incidence of mental disorders, specifically psychosis

14

(Hollingshead and Redlich, 1958; Langner and Michael, 1968; Leighton et al., 1962).

Lack of Psychological research. Specific research on the Mexican American's mental health is practically nonexistent. Many factors contribute toward the difficulty of providing this population with much needed psychological services: i.e., the lack of psychological research, the failure of the Mexican American to use existing public inpatient and outpatient services, the psycho-social heterogeneity of their culture and their lack of English language fluency. For example, the prevalence of mental illness among this population has only been studied superficially (Jaco, 1959) and the socio-economic characteristics of Mexican Americans who have specific types of mental illness is not known: nor has the effectiveness of various psychotherapeutic modalities been tested scientifically with this population. Furthermore, the available research concerning the relationship between poverty and the incidence of mental illness cannot be generalized to the Mexican American because this research has been primarily based on Anglo and/or Black populations.

Their failure to use services. This population's consistent failure to use existing public inpatient and outpatient psychiatric facilities prevents the study of the relative effectiveness of these services with the Mexican American. During the 12-month period of 1969 to 1970, Mexican American admissions to California state mental hospitals represented only 2.65 percent of the total admissions (California Department of Mental Hygiene, 1970). Jaco (1959), Karno (1965), Karno and Edgerton (1969), and Torrey (1970) report similar under-representations for the states of California and Texas. Jaco (1959) attributes this under-representation to this population's low incidence of psychosis due to the Mexican American's "subcultural system," i.e., close family ties etc., while Karno (1965) attributes to it "... the intensity and variety of conflict in expectation which occur when the unacculturated

15

Mexican American encounters traditional Anglo medical institutions (p. 519)." At the same time, Karno and Edgerton (1969) failed to find support for their hypothesis that the Mexican Americans' under-representation was due to the difference in their perceptions and definitions of and their responses to, mental illness. The inaccessible locations of psychiatric facilities, their lack of bilingual professional staffs, their use of inappropriate treatment models, and their failure to employ Mexican American ombudsmen and curanderas (faith healers) is the reason why this population fails to use existing services according to Torrey (1970). Opler (1967) provides still another explanation. He states: "Ethnic or cultural distance combined with lower class status, insulates the lower class from the needed forms of psychotherapeutic care (p. 279)." And, Riessman (1967) points out that the refusal of the poor to use inappropriate services is their essential power, the power of the veto.

The heterogeneity of the Mexican American in particular contributes to the difficulty of tailoring psychological services for this population. The importance of this factor is supported by this investigator's several years of clinical practice as well as by the findings of Grebler, et al. (1970) and Peñalosa (1967, 1970). Grebler et al., state: "Certainly, the Mexican American culture is not now an integrated whole. Eroded, altered, and shifted by its exposure to the American experience, it has been transformed into an amalgam (p. 423)." According to Peñalosa (1967), "Existentially there is no Mexican American community as such, nor is there such a 'thing' as Mexican American culture. The group is fragmentized socially, ideologically, and organizationally. It is characterized by extremely important social-class, regional, and rural-urban differences (p. 406)." Peñalosa (1970) states further "... our subject is not at all simple, but exceedingly complex. Mexican Americans may constitute one of the most heterogeneous ethnic groups ever to be studied by sociologists (p. 1)."

In addition to his cultural heterogeneity, the Mexican American may differ in other variables. His skin color may range from querito (blond), triqueñito (light brown), prietito (dark brown), to negrito (black). His Spanish and English fluency may vary, as well as the type of Spanish he speaks. He may speak flawless Castilian, correct Mexican Spanish, or some variant of Spanish such as that spoken in California called Pochismo. His identification with Mexico may vary as well as his nativity. Heterogeneity can also characterize his occupational, political, economic, and acculturational attainments.

The importance of considering the Mexican American's bilingualism when rendering psychological services is emphasized in the literature (cf: Karno, 1965; Morales, 1971; Karno and Morales, 1971; Opler, 1967). Karno (1965), for example, suggests that the staff's failure to attend to the Mexican American's ethnicity and bilingualism may be related to this population's failure to use mental health services. Morales (1971) similarly feels that his clinical experience demonstrates that Mexican American patients are more at ease when they are able to communicate in their own language. In addition, Karno and Morales (1971) strongly assert that "... Mexican American patients respond at least as well as their Anglo counterparts when they are offered professionally expert treatment in a context of cultural and linguistic familiarity and acceptance (p. 284)." That knowledge of the client's language and subcultural group is an essential prerequisite to rendering psychological services is further supported by Opler (1967).

Even though research is very limited in this area, there is some evidence to suggest that differences in language usage is related to socio-economic class differences among Mexican Americans. Grebler et al., (1970) found English linguistic competence to be positively correlated to income. Similar evidence is provided by Karno and Edgerton (1969) who found that 40 percent of their low income Mexican American respondents spoke only or mainly Spanish. Glazer (1966) also notes the paradox of the extraordinary language loyalty of the Mexican American of the Southwest and their extraordinary poverty.

Language usage may also be related to other characteristics which may have psychotherapeutic implications. Edgerton and Karno (1971) studied a large randomly selected sample of Mexican Americans of East Los Angeles. In their search for variables which might be related to differences in perception of, and response to mental illness, they found no significant differences with such variables as age, sex, religion, amount of education, type of occupation, and number of years of residence in the United States. They found, however, that the best predictor among all possible variables was simply the language spoken during the interview. Variation in language preference was found not only to be related to differences in perception of, and response to mental illness, but also to differences in a cluster of other characteristics. Those who preferred Spanish were found to be monolingual, older, more frequently Mexico-born, less educated, more frequently unemployed, more regular in church attendance and more concerned with religion, more frequent viewers and listeners of Spanish language television and Spanish language radio programs, respectively, and more frequent readers of Spanish language newspapers. Those who preferred English were found to be bilingual, younger, more frequently native-born, better educated, more frequently employed, less regular in church attendance and less concerned with religion, and less frequent viewers and listeners of Spanish language television and Spanish language radio programs, respectively, and less frequent readers of Spanish language newspapers.

English fluency may not only serve as a reliable predictor of socio-economic and other differences, but may also provide an index of acculturation into the majority, i.e., more Anglo-American culture. Haugen (1956) states: "The immigrant is being gradually integrated into the main cultural stream of his country; as the anthropologists put it, he is being acculturated whether he wishes or not. This process finds its expression in his language, first by the changes it undergoes, and second by the gradual restrictions of its use (p. 28.)" Tharp, Meadow, Lennhoff and

Satterfield (1968) in their study of Mexican American wives of Tucson, Arizona noted that English fluency was correlated with several indicators of assimilation, i.e., higher levels of education, birth in the United States, and residence in ethnically mixed neighborhoods. Not only are linguistic ability and social acculturation related but it would appear that they may be part of a self-reinforcing cycle. Low English competency very likely may restrict the individual to isolated low paying work and to low income housing which is often substandard and segregated. This phenomenon in itself is self perpetuating; these limited linguistic and acculturational opportunities influence his low English and acculturational levels and these in turn promote his poverty.

Given the factors of the Mexican American's pervasive poverty, his heterogeneity of social, psychological and cultural backgrounds and his varying degrees of bilingualism, psychological services as currently formulated and administered may have little or no relevance to this population's needs. One reason for this irrelevancy may well be the type of psychological services rendered. Psychological services, for the most part, are based primarily on approaches to therapy which do not take into consideration specific differences among clients. The same general therapy models are used with individuals regardless of their ethnic, socio-economic, or personal backgrounds. If therapy is to be effective it would seem that it should be focused on and take into consideration the client himself and include the environmental and cultural factors that shape his particular behaviors. The Mexican American's bilingualism and his poverty are two such factors.

Role playing and modeling. One such therapeutic technique which is easily modified to meet specific client needs is that of role playing and social modeling. Role playing is described by Krumboltz and Thoresen (1969) as having many variants and as consisting "... of a client practicing some behavior he wants to learn in a situation where errors he makes will not be ridiculed or punished in any way (p. 79)." This procedure is most effective

19

when performed under realistic situations and when the counselor reinforces correctly demonstrated behaviors. Social modeling, on the other hand, involves demonstration of the desired behavior by a model which is followed by the observation and imitation by the subject (Krumboltz and Thoresen, 1969). Four interrelated processes present in the modeling procedure are: attentional, retentional, motoric reproduction, and reinforcement-motivational process (cf: Bandura, 1971). These procedures, common to both modeling and role playing strategies, do not require verbal fluency nor the cognitive ability which are essential aspects of most traditional therapies.

The low socio-economic Mexican American in particular, may not only be limited in English fluency but may not be able to perform cognitively, nor conceptualize psychologically to the extent required by the traditional psychotherapy. In addition, this population may use a restricted linguistic code which is concommitant to the culture of poverty, i.e., speech which is explicit, here and now, rigid, narrow, particularistic and extra verbally oriented (Bernstein, 1964, 1970). Role playing and modeling are action oriented strategies which appear to be un-affected by and, at the same time, may specifically utilize the restricted linguistic code of this population.

Riessman and Goldfarb (1964) provide four additional reasons for utilizing role playing techniques with such types of clients:

1. It appears congenial with the low income persons's style which is physical (action oriented, doing vs. talking; down to earth concrete, problem directed; externally ori-ented rather than introspective; group centered; game-like rather than test oriented; easy and informal in tempo.

2. It allows the practitioner (social worker, psychia-trist, educator) to reduce in an honest fashion the role distance between himself and the disadvantaged individual who is often alienated from him. It also permits the practitioner to learn more about the culture of the low

income person from the inside (through playing the latter's role in role reversal).

3. It changes the setting and tone of what often appear to be to the low income person, an office ridden, bureaucratic, impersonal, foreign world,

4. It appears to be an excellent technique for developing verbal power in the educationally deprived person, who is said to be largely inarticulate. Moreover, it seems to be especially useful for the development of leadership skills (pp. 339-340).

Shaffer (1968) as well as Nelson (1968) similarly support the use of a role playing variant of traditional analytic therapy, "paradigmatic psychotherapy," in which the therapist uses strategically selected types of role playing and modeling. Shaffer bases his support for the use of this approach for low income clients on its reliance on role playing which emphasizes the experiencing--as opposed to the analysis--of feelings; the opportunity to reflect back to the patient attitudes from others that he experiences in his day-to-day life; and the availability of multiple role behaviors.

In addition, modeling procedures have been found to be specially effective with subjects who demonstrate lack of self esteem (de Charms and Rosenbaum, 1960; Gelfand, 1962), feelings of incompetence (Kanariff and Lanzetta, 1960), and dependency (Jakubezuk and Walters, 1959; Ross, 1966). These characteristics are likely to be common to the low income individual in general and to the low income Mexican American in specific. Still further, role playing and modeling procedures consider the low income person's expectation for an active yet permissive therapist (Overall and Aronson, 1964), his need for assistance delivered in a direct, forthright manner (McMahon, 1964), and his need for structured, definite and specific interview content (Riessman and Goldfarb, 1964).

The tremendous lack of bilingual professionals makes it

necessary to choose treatment modalities which could be easily learned by beginning counselors as well as other resource persons. Bandura (1971) specifically recommends the utilization of resource persons in modeling procedures rather than professional personnel. This recommendation is especially meaningful because of the tremendous lack of bilingual professional staff.

A relatively new behavioral counseling model which combines role playing and social modeling strategies is entitled "Behavior Rehearsal" by Lazarus (1966) and "Behavioristic Psychodrama" by Wolpe (1958, 1969). Behavior Rehearsal is recommended for: (1) substituting effective behaviors which are absent or inefficient (Lazarus, 1966); (2) deconditioning anxiety and establishing motor assertive habits (Wolpe, 1969); and (3)enhancing motor skills, information storage or imprinting a pattern of social usage (Urban and Ford, 1971). As is generally true of role playing and modeling strategies, Behavior Rehearsal has been credited with much success but controlled outcome studies are nonexistant (Bandura, 1971). Additional studies comparing the therapeutic effectiveness of Behavior Rehearsal with a contrasting treatment modality is urgently needed.

Therapeutic Listening. The type of therapy most common in traditional mental health programs is insight therapy, in which Therapeutic Listening is the predominant technique of the therapist. Therapeutic Listening, to be effective, requires that the client be able to verbalize fluently and interpret his feelings and emotions in such a way that the counselor can assist him in gaining insight into his problem. Therapeutic Listening is a part of Rogers' (1942) client-centered therapy which seeks to modify the client's problems through the mechanisms of insight and catharsis. Insight, according to Rogers (1942), implies the perception of new meaning in the individual's own experience. To see new relationships of cause and effect, to gain new understanding of the meaning which behavior symptoms have had, to understand the patterning of one's behavior--such learnings constitute insight (p. 174)." The development of insight, Rogers relates, involves not only the recognition of the role which the individual is playing as well as the recognition of repressed impulses within the self. Catharsis, an important part of gaining insight, is the emotional release or the expression of emotionally loaded material. Rogers (1942) compares catharsis to the Catholic Church's use of confession which allows the individual to ventilate his difficulties under the condition of counselor acceptance. The phenomenon supposedly frees the individual from conscious fears and guilt feelings and brings to light the more deeply buried attitudes which influence behavior (Rogers, 1942).

Therapeutic Listening is also an important aspect of several other currently used therapies such as Jackin's Re-evaluation Counseling (1965). Jackin's asserts that the client's natural self-healing faculties take place when the counselor is warm, accepting, relaxed and attentive. On the other hand, verbalizing, interpreting, sympathizing, and analyzing are seen as behaviors which interfere with the healing process. Bergman (1951) similarly points out that the therpist's structuring and interpretation are usually followed by the client's decline in self-exploration while self-exploration continues after reflection by the therapist. Ruesch (1960) states that such traditional counseling models encourage the counselor to sort, label, and classify the client's communication. These attempts to dissect the client's message prevents the counselor from subjectively experiencing the impact of the client's communication. Thus, results are often distorted and understanding impaired. Therefore, while Therapeutic Listening and insight are both essential aspects of traditional psychotherapy, there is little evidence to support the effectiveness of these counseling techniques with low socioeconomic Mexican Americans. Nor has this therapeutic procedure been compared experimentally with more active types of therapy, e.g., Behavior Rehearsal, with this population. Research is badly needed in this area if the Mexican American is to benefit from mental health services offered by the community.

Summary

    The disadvantaged position of the Mexican American has been utilized to document their urgent need for appropriate psychological services. Multiple factors which contribute to the enormous difficulty in providing such services have been defined and discussed. The significance of providing psychological services which take into consideration the Mexican American's unique characteristics, especially his poverty and the various degrees of his bilingualism was strongly emphasized. Such a treatment modality would have to have the flexibility of serving the Mexican American with his cultural, linguistic, occupational, political, psychological and economic heterogeneity.

    Behavior Rehearsal, a counseling strategy which combines role playing and social modeling procedures was described. Evidence in support of the premise that this treatment modality may be suited to the needs of the Mexican American was provided. A contrasting treatment procedure, Therapeutic Listening, was presented. This variant of Roger's nondirective therapy and Jackin's Re-evaluation Counseling was described as a counseling technique common to most traditional psychotherapy carried out in mental facilities today. This model's essential therapeutic aspects include catharsis and insight, both of which require psychological conceptualization and an elaborated linguistic code. These requirements were seen as handicapping to the Mexican American who is likely to be poor and thus limited in his cognitive flexibility and his ability to conceptualize psychologically in ways which most presently practicing therapists can understand and utilize in the therapy process. The Mexican American's limited English vocabulary as well as his restricted linguistic code also serve to attentuate the effect of therapy. Thus this study proposes to test the use of Therapeutic Listening and Behavioral Rehearsal in helping Mexican Americans solve psychological conflicts for which they seek counseling.

24

NOTES

[1]The term Mexican American, as used in this study, signifies a person of Mexican heritage regardless of liberal or conservative political affiliation.

[2]The term Anglo is operationally defined as a White non-Spanish surnamed person.

[3]The term Nonwhite is used according to the 1960 U.S. census to include Afro-Americans, Indians and Orientals. When used to refer to Texas populations this term will signify only Afro-Americans.

CHAPTER II

EXPERIMENTAL DESIGN AND PROCEDURE

Overview of the Study

The main purpose of this study was to compare and test experimentally the therapeutic effectiveness of two individual counseling strategies, Therapeutic Listening and Behavior Rehearsal, with Mexican Americans at the low socio-economic level. Therapeutic Listening, a treatment procedure developed specifically for this study, is a variant of Roger's (1942) client-centered therapy and Jackin's (1965) Re-evaluation Counseling. This treatment procedure utilizes the therapeutic mechanisms of insight and catharsis; Behavior Rehearsal, a role playing and social modeling technique, utilizes demonstration, graduated enactment, behavioral prescriptions and systematic positive reinforcement. In order to control for the variable of sex, only women were used as subjects of the study.

More specifically, this study sought to determine which of these two counseling procedures was more effective in promoting the desired outcomes, e.g., attainment of client-specific goals and attendance at therapy. The criteria for the specification and measurement of therapeutic outcomes were the pre- and post-assessments of five problems elicited by the investigator from each subject at the initial interview. Attendance in therapy was used as one of the dependent variables. The independent variable was the exposure to one of two counseling treatment procedures - Therapeutic Listening and Behavior Rehearsal.

The study used a "Pretest-posttest Group Design" recommended by Campbell and Stanley (1963, p. 13) for educational and psychological research. Randomization procedures were utilized to assign each subject to one of the two treatment conditions and to one of the three counselors.

Unique Aspects of the Study

This study is unique in the area of counseling research for several reasons:

1. Research testing the effectiveness of an insight counseling model with a behavioral action oriented model has not been attempted with low income Mexican American women.

2. Counseling research utilizing bilingual (English and Spanish) counselors who use the subject's language preference during the counseling sessions has not been carried out with low income Mexican American women.

3. Counseling services, delivered in a context of cultural familiarity and combined with needed auxilliary services such as transportation, baby-sitting, and referral to other agencies also have not been tested with this population.

Questions and Hypotheses

Based on the review of the literature and the clinical experience of the investigator for which rationales have been presented in Chapter 1, the following research questions and hypotheses were formulated for testing:

1. What are the ethnic, socio-economic and personal characteristics of Mexican American women who volunteered for the special counseling services of the study?

2. What problem categories are most frequently presented during the initial intake interviews?

3. To what problem areas do low socio-economic Mexican American women address themselves most frequently during counseling sessions?

4. Which type of referral sources are most effective in motivating low socio-economic Mexican American women to seek counseling?

5. How important is the provision of auxilliary services, e.g., transportation, baby-sitting, to this population's seeking and continuing in counseling?

In addition, the following experimental hypotheses were tested:

27

1. Subjects exposed to Behavior Rehearsal will demonstrate more favorable therapeutic outcomes as measured by post assessment on the Goal Attainment Scale than will subjects exposed to Therapeutic Listening.

2. Subjects exposed to Behavior Rehearsal will attend counseling sessions more frequently than will subjects exposed to Therapeutic Listening.

3. The relationship between treatment attendance and therapeutic outcome will be positive.

4. The subjects will more frequently prefer to speak Spanish than English during the counseling sessions.

Subjects

The subjects for this study were low-income Mexican American women residing in Ventura County, California; attaining 20 years or more in age; coming from homes of annual per capita income of less than $2,000 and volunteering for counseling services. Individuals judged by this investigator during the initial interview to require hospitalization, to be serious suicide risks, to be acutely psychotic or to have a history of Organic Brain Disease were excluded from the sample. Observations, clinical records, and client reports were used for this purpose. Also eliminated were those women who were Spanish surnamed but not of Mexican ancestry. Thirty-six subjects who met these specifications were utilized in the study.

Several methods were employed to recruit subjects: (1) a letter written in English and Spanish (Appendix A) was sent to 200 mothers whose children attended a summer Neighborhood Youth Corps program; to ten or more professionals and para-professionals with large Mexican American case loads (e.g., Welfare, Public Health, Legal Aid, Probation, Mental Health agencies); and to 100 private homes in neighborhoods with a high density of low income Mexican Americans; (2) announcements were made in Spanish on a local Spanish radio station; (3) English and Spanish articles were published in a local Spanish newspaper; and (4) community leaders were contacted by the investigator by letter, or in person when possible, to engage their assistance in referring appropriate clients.

Women desiring counseling were instructed to call a local phone number and ask for a specific, bilingual, male, mental health para-professional. This worker noted the person's name and phone number and language preference for counseling, and gave her an appointment for an intake interview with the investigator.

Experimental Setting

The setting for this study was the Community Service Center (CSO) of Oxnard, California. Since its inception in 1959, this center has been operated for and by residents of "LaColonia" (Colony or Mexican American Neighborhood). It has had the advantage of being very well known to and accepted by the low income Mexican American residents of Oxnard. In addition, its location is central to low income neighborhoods and to well known community agencies such as Neighborhood Youth Corps, Public Health Clinic and Mexican American Opportunity Center. Unfortunately, the physical facilities reflected the poverty of the community, e.g., the three office spaces used by the counselors were made by dividing a large, drafty room with three makeshift partitions. Thus, the physical conditions, especially the acoustics, were less than ideal as complete confidentiality was not always possible to maintain during the counseling sessions.

Counselor Selection and Training

After a considerable search, three female counselors were selected for the study. Selection was guided by the following criteria: (1) familiarity with the culture of the Mexican American and of the poor; (2) verbal fluencing in English and Spanish; (3) aptitude for and desire to do counseling; (4) graduation from college; and (5) chronological maturity of 30 years or older.

The investigator utilized two six-hour sessions to train the counselors in the specific treatment conditions. Six hours of discussions and role playing were used for each treatment modality.

Counselor behaviors appropriate for each treatment condition were specified, discussed and demonstrated. Each counselor was encouraged to demonstrate these behaviors while another counselor role played a client in need of counseling. The counselors discussed and demonstrated the specified counselor behaviors in English, Spanish and a mixture of Spanish and English. Attempts were made to recall authentic counseling situations which depicted Mexican American women. These situations were role played and the counselors practiced responses specific to the Behavior Rehearsal and Therapeutic Listening counseling models.

Behavior Rehearsal. The investigator introduced Behavior Rehearsal to the counselors as a relatively new behavior strategy useful for teaching behaviors which were either absent from the subjects' behavioral repertoire or present in insufficient intensity. This action technique utilized the specification and demonstration of needed behaviors by the counselor and the gradual practice of these behaviors by the subject under the counselor's guidance and reinforcement. The following dialogue is an example of counselor responses appropriate to this strategy:

Mrs. B_____ is a poorly educated, native born Mexican American who speaks only Spanish. She is sixty years of age and has been married three times. Her most serious target complaint was her desire to kill her 30 year old husband who had left her for a younger woman.

Counselor: Mrs. B_____, you need to practice controlling your anger in order to prevent physical violence from destroying your life and that of your husband. I would like to help you learn how to do this. Are you watching me carefully, so that you can imitate what I do?

Mrs. B____: Yeah.

Counselor: O.K. Let's pretend that I am you and that I see Joe, my husband walking arm in arm with his girl friend. I start to feel very angry. As soon as I feel this anger I say to myself "Stop -- he is not worth it." I walk away.

Mrs. B____ : I don't want to walk away. I want to at least scratch his face with a bobby pin.

Counselor: No, I want you to imitate what I demonstrated. O.K. Now, you remember what I did. You do it.

Mrs. B.___ : O.K. I'll do it.

Counselor: Good for you. You did a good job. Let me demonstrate this again so that you can practice it again. This time walk away from him sooner and don't provoke him by your loud cursing.

Mrs. B____ : But I feel like telling that motherless wetback that he is a no good _____.

Counselor: O.K. I'll demonstrate you seeing him, walking away and cursing after he is out of sight.

This example was provided to illustrate the importance of modeling behavior which the subject could accept, imitate and utilize.

Therapeutic Listening. Therapeutic Listening was introduced as a traditional counseling procedure whose central feature was the facilitation of catharsis and insight by the counselor's attentive, accepting and non-interfering responses. The following dialogue utilizes the same subject described in the Behavior Rehearsal example and illustrates counselor responses specific to this counseling model:

Mrs. B____ . Everytime I see them together I see red. I get so angry I wish I could kill them both.

Counselor: You feel they've made a fool of you?

Mrs. B___ : Well, how would you feel? I spent hundreds of dollars in fixing his immigration papers. He said he loved me and would always be faithful. Now look how he treats me.

Counselor: It's hard controlling your anger when you feel so hurt?

Mrs. B____ : Yes I feel hurt. I feel hurt and foolish. I guess they are right when they say there is no fool like an old fool (starts to cry).

This dialogue illustrated the main therapeutic mechanism of this counseling model - the facilitation of catharsis and insight which could be utilized by a relatively poorly educated individual.

Initial Interview

The initial subject contact was an intake interview conducted by the investigator in the same setting selected for the counseling This individual intake interview consisted of the investigator providing:

1. Friendly greeting in the subject's preferred language and offer of coffee and pastry.

2. Brief explanation of the purposes of the counseling.

3. Explanation and signature of a research consent form (Appendix B).

4. Administration of an Initial Questionnaire (Appendix C).

5. Encouragement for the subject as she discussed her problems.

6. Summarization and review of these problems with the subject.

7. Practical advice as warranted by the subject's urgent need for assistance.

8. Encouragement to attend the counseling sessions.

9. Referral to existing auxiliary services if needed, e.g., public health, welfare, etc.

10. Termination of the interview.

11. Random assignment for next interview to counselor and treatment.

12. Summarization and listing of the client's problems for the assigned counselor (Appendix D).

13. Selection and scaling of five client specific problems according to the specification of the Goal Attainment Scale (Appendix E).

Pre-Treatment Assessment

During the initial intake interview the subjects were asked

to discuss the reasons which led them to seek counseling, and from these discussions the investigator determined five mental health problems for each subject. These target complaints were given general labels such as "Depression: brooding thoughts," "Depression: unresolved grief," "Relationship to son: limit setting," "Relationship to husband: physical aggression," "Nutrition: overweight," etc. These labeled problem areas were then ranked by the investigator in terms of their importance to the subject's mental health. The Goal Attainment Scale (GAS), an instrument developed by the Hennepin County, Minnesota Mental Health Center (Kiresuk, 1970; Kiresuk and Sherman, 1968), was utilized for the purpose of pre-treatment selecting, labeling, ranking, and scaling of these subject specific problems and for their post-treatment assessment. This scale was designed specifically for use by para-professionals and other workers with minimal training to do post-treatment assessments of client progress relative to treatment (Appendix E provides a copy of the Goal Attainment Scale).

After the subject's problems were identified, labeled and ranked, each was scaled by the investigator into five possible treatment outcomes. These five prognostic indicators or goal attainments ranged from the "most unfavorable treatment outcomes thought possible" (given a -2 value) to the "most favorable treatment outcome thought possible" (given a +2 value). Thus, the prognostic indicators for each goal were: most unfavorable treatment outcome thought likely (-2), less than expected success with treatment (-1), expected level of treatment success (0), more than expected success with treatment (+1) and most favorable treatment outcome thought likely (+2). For example, a subject may have indicated five target complaints. These the investigator labeled and ranked from most to least important to the subject's mental health (Table 13) and then behaviorally described them in terms of five possible levels of attainment, ranging from most unfavorable to most favorable (Table 14 provides an example of this procedure). Following the specification of the five levels of goal attainment for each problem which the subject described, the investigator determined the level which best described each problem that the subject presented at the intake interview. This level was marked with one asterisk (Table 14). When all the five target complaints were labeled, ranked and scaled, randomization procedures were utilized to assign each subject to eight sessions in one of two treatment conditions with one of three bilingual female counselors. Table 15 provides a schematic diagram of the procedure in which subjects were assigned to treatment.

TABLE 13

Goal Attainment Follow-Up Guide
(Five Target Complaints)

	Scale Headings and Scale Weights		
Levels of Predicted Attainment	Scale 1 Relationship to Husbands: Control his physical aggression	Scale 2 Relationship to Children: Encourage Communication	Scale 3 Psychosomatic Symptoms
	Scale 4 Depression: Brooding Thoughts	Scale 5 Occupation: Lack of Work and/or Training	

34

TABLE 14

Goal Attainment Follow-up Guide
(Five Levels of Attainment)

	Scale Headings & Scale Weights		
Levels of Predicted Attainment	Scale 1 Relationship to Husband: Control His Physical Aggression	Scale 2 Relationship to Children: Encourage Communication	Scale 3 Psychosomatic Symptoms
Most un-favorable outcome thought likely (-2)	Aggression will become more fre-quent or more severe. She may be killed or seriously injured		
Less than expected success (-1)	*At least once every 2 weeks husband beats her; facial and body bruising, broken finger, injured shoulder		
Expected level of success (0)	Will take some action to protect self; lock self in room, leave house,		
More than expected success (+1)	Will take more as-sertive action; call police and file charges		
Most fa-vorable outcome thought likely (+2)	**Aggression will stop or she will get legal separa-tion from husband		

*Indicates present be-havior at intake; assessed by investigator

**Indicates present behavior at follow-up; assessed by follow-up worker

Scale 4
Depression brooding thoughts

Scale 5
Occupation: Lack of work and/or training

TABLE 15

Subject Assignment Procedures

	Subjects Volunteering	
	N = 36	
Random Assignment to Three Counselors Trained in Both Treatment Conditions		
Counselor A (12 Ss)	Counselor M (12 Ss)	Counselor M (12 Ss)
Random Assignment to Therapy Conditions	Random Assignment to Therapy Conditions	Random Assignment to Therapy Conditions
Therapeutic Behavior Rehearsal / Therapeutic Listening	Therapeutic Behavior Rehearsal / Therapeutic Listening	Therapeutic Behavior Rehearsal / Therapeutic Listening
N = 6 N = 6	N = 6 N = 6	N = 6 N = 6

36

goal attainment for each problem which the subject described, the
investigator determined the level which best described each problem that the subject presented at the intake interview. This
level was marked with one asterisk (Table 14). When all the five
target complaints were labeled, ranked and scaled, randomization
procedures were utilized to assign each subject to eight sessions
in one of two treatment conditions with one of three bilingual
female counselors. Table 15 provides a schematic diagram of the
procedure in which subjects were assigned to treatment.

Auxilliary Services

The selection of an individual who provided the auxilliary
services was guided by the following criteria: (1) familiarity
with the culture of the Mexican American and the poor; (2) verbal
fluency in English and Spanish; (3) experience in community work;
(4) familiarity with the Ventura County low income Mexican American
neighborhoods; (5) possession of a valid driver's license and car
insurance and (6) chronological maturity of 30 years or more. The
investigator utilized six, 30-minute sessions to instruct this individual concerning her specific duties and the importance of her
role to the study. Additionally, phone calls and personal communi-
cations were provided by the investigator as needed throughout the
study. Specifically the auxilliary services worker was asked to:

(1) Announce to Mexican American community groups the
availability of counseling.

(2) Maintain a warm, interested relationship with the subjects
of the study but to avoid discussions specific to their therapy.

(3) Make weekly counseling appointments for the subjects
and keep an orderly appointment book.

(4) Call all subjects missing a scheduled appointment and
encourage them to attend counseling on a regular basis.

(5) provide all subjects with transportation and baby-sitting
as requested.

(6) Maintain confidentiality.

(7) Tell subjects of existing community services and make appointments as needed.

(8) Schedule appointments for the subjects with the post-assessment interviewer.

(9) Help improve the comfort of the treatment setting.

(10) Buy pastry and make coffee as needed during the counseling sessions.

Selection and Training of the Post-assessment Interviewer

Criteria used for the selection of the post-assessment interviewer consisted of: (1) familiarity with the culture of the Mexican American and of the poor; (2) verbal fluencing in English and Spanish; (3) interviewing experience and (4) chronological maturity of 30 years or more. One individual, a Mexican American woman, was selected to conduct the post-assessment interview. The investigator utilized two sessions of two hours each to train this worker in the use of the Goal Attainment Scale for the post-treatment assessment of the therapeutic outcome. The Program Instruction in Goal Attainment Scaling (Hennepin County, 1971) was used for this purpose. After completing the instructional material, discussion and role playing sessions were held using sample GAS ratings. This worker was not connected with the study in any other way nor was she informed of the counselor or treatment assignment of the subjects or the frequency of their attendance at counseling.

Post-treatment Assessment

All clients were scheduled for post-treatment assessments during a period of eight to ten weeks from the initial intake interview. Due to multiple complications in setting up appointments, e.g., frequent trips to Mexico, illness in the family, etc., the assessments were rescheduled for eight to twelve weeks from pre-assessment. Utilizing the Goal Attainment Scale previously specified for each subject by the investigator, the post-assessment interviewer determined the current attainment level for each subject's target complaints. This setermination was made by the evaluator asking the subject to discuss each of the five previously specified target complaints in terms of the subject's present level of functioning. For example, a target complaint labeled "Relationship with husband: physical aggression" might be assessed by reviewing the GAS illustrated in Table 14 and by saying to the subject:

Evaluator: I am Mrs. D____. Your counselor has discussed with you my purpose in coming to see you. I would like to take a few minutes of your time to see how you are doing in relation to the problems which you mentioned when you first came for counseling. One of the problems which you mentioned was that about every two weeks your husband was physically beating you in the face and body. Could you tell me how often he has beaten you since you have started counseling?

Subject: You know it's not right for a human being to take so much abuse. My husband drinks a lot but that should not excuse his nasty behavior.

Evaluator: Can you remember how many times he has beaten you since you started counseling?

Subject: Well, let me see, I started counseling in January and since then he got drunk several times and went right into his nasty, mean behavior.

Evaluator: Did he beat you three times since January?

Subject: No, he did not beat me at all. He tried to but I did not argue with him. I just took my kids and went to my mother's house.

Evaluator: O.K., let me mark this (places double asterisk at "expected level of success" (O) on GAS and then continues her inquiry concerning the subject's other four target complaints).

Treatment Conditions

The counselors were given a brief written description of each subject by the investigator who conducted the interview. This included a list of the problems which the client presented (an example of a summary used is found in Appendix D). Additionally, the investigator reviewed this information individually with each counselor prior to the subject's first counseling session. The counselors were further instructed to encourage all subjects to attend eight, 45-minute counseling sessions.

Therapeutic Listening. The two therapy models, Therapeutic Listening and Behavior Rehearsal described in Chapter I, were employed as the experimental treatments. The counselors utilizing the Therapeutic Listening model were instructed to:

1. Greet the subject warmly, in their preferred language and offer her coffee and pastry. The use of simple, down to earth, folksy expressions were encouraged, e.g., "Good morning, Mrs. S., I am Mrs. R., your counselor. May I serve you some coffee and pastry? Here is our office space, please make yourself comfortable." Or, similarly in Spanish: "Buenos dias Senora S. Yo soy la Senora R., su consejera. Le siervo una tacita de cafe y pan dulce? Aqui esta nuestra oficina, sientese por favor."

2. Explain the counselor behaviors appropriate for this treatment model, e.g., "I would like to take a few minutes to explain to you how I might be of help. I will primarily give you my undivided attention, listen to your difficulties and try to understand them. I will encourage you to find ways of solving your problems."

Further the counselors were instructed to avoid:

1. Making comments which were sympathetic, analytic or interpretive.

2. Asking questions concerning causality, but instead phrase questions as polite, interested comments such as "Tell me more about ..." or similarly in Spanish "Hagame el favor de darme mas detelles acerca de ..."

3. Probing into areas not initiated by the subject.

4. Excessive counselor verbalization.

In addition, the counselors were to:

1. Assist the subject in understanding what she is or was feeling by asking problem solving types of questions such as "What are you feeling inside? How did you feel when this happened? What did you want to do?"

2. Encourage the subject to feel understood by using the various forms of acknowledgment recommended by Ruesch (1957) such as "I heard what you said and I think I understand. You were saying that ..."

3. Clarify what is being said by the using of paraphrasing.

4. Respond to the client's request for information with simple brief statements.

Paraphrasing in this study was defined as the process which the counselor used to communicate his understanding and to elicit further discussion, e.g., "In other words, you are saying that you've just simply had it with your husband. That you can't take his cruelty any longer?" Or, similarly in Spanish "Lo que Ud. me esta diciendo en otras palabras es que Ud. ya no le puede aguantar a su esposo, que ya no puede soportar su crueldad?"

Behavior Rehearsal. The counselors employing the Behavior Rehearsal treatment strategy were instructed to:

1. Greet the subject warmly in her preferred language and offer her coffee and pastry.

2. Explain the counselor behaviors appropriate for this treatment model, e.g., "I would like to take a few minutes to explain to you how I might be of help. I will attempt to listen to your problems in order to help you determine what we can do about them and specifically how I can help you learn to do things differently. I will demonstrate how to act in different ways and encourage you to practice these new ways so that you can solve your problems.

3. Determine specific behaviors which the subject needs to learn. For example, one subject might need to learn to speak more firmly to her children in order to control their misbehavior.

4. Discuss the needed behavior with the subject and impress upon the client her need for learning this behavior.

5. Demonstrate by example and role playing at a level which the subject can successfully imitate.

6. Encourage the subject to imitate the behavior which has been demonstrated. Continue this practice until the subject

41

successfully approximates the learned behavior.

7. Utilize systematic approval to encourage the subject to continue to practice the needed behavior.

8. Assign the practice of the behavior in the subject's home and/or work situation. The counselors were cautioned to avoid assigning this practice under conditions which might yield negative consequences. For example, a woman with an explosive, physically violent husband would not be encouraged to practice asser- tive verbalizations with him.

Treatment Reliability

All counseling sessions conducted by each counselor in both of the treatment conditions were tape recorded when the subject gave her permission. These tapes were then evaluated by bilingual counselors-in-training who were otherwise not associated with the study in order to insure that the experimental conditions were, in fact, carried out according to the specified models. The criterion used for this evaluation was a Rating Scale (Appendix F) which measured whether certain counselor behaviors specific to each of the two experimental counseling conditions were demonstrated. Utilizing randomization procedures, two tapes for each counselor in both of the treatment groups were selected for determining inter- judge reliability. The bilingual raters listened to the first thirty minutes of each tape and rated specific counselor responses relative to the specified evaluation form. Inter-judge reliability of these two raters was established using the Kendall tau coef- ficient (Hays, 1963). High rater concordance was found for each of the five sections of the Rating Scale (r_1 = .66, r_2 = 1, r_4 - 1, r_5 = 1).

Measurement of Dependent Variables

The major dependent variable in this study was the treatment outcomes as specified and measured by the Goal Attainment Scale pre- and post-treatment assessments. Additionally, the subjects' frequency of attendance at therapy and the promptness of their arrival were recorded by their counselors. Other variables which might have psychotherapeutic implications were also assessed. The subjects' ethnic, socio-economic and personal characteristics were assessed by utilizing the data collected with the Initial Intake Questionnaire (Appendix C). This questionnaire interview tool was constructed so that research questions number one, four and five could be tested. The constructed data collecting tool was submitted to two experts in counseling research. After the necessary revisions were made, it was administered to a small group of Mexican American women, currently attending individual therapy with the investigator at Santa Barbara County Mental Health Services. It was found that additional revisions were not necessary (Appendix C).

In addition, research question two was tested by the utilization of the Goal Attainment Scale which facilitated the specification of five target complaints. Research question number three was assessed by instructing the counselors to summarize after each counseling session the problem areas discussed by the subject. A content analysis was carried out in the counselor's summaries to determine which problem areas were most frequently discussed.

CHAPTER III

RESULTS

This chapter presents an analysis of results obtained for each hypothesis and research question which, for the sake of clarity, will be summarized individually. A 3 x 2 analysis of variance was made for disproportionate subclass frequencies of the data (Winer, 1971) with the type of treatment model and counselor as main effects; interaction between these independent variables was also analyzed. Statistical computations were made using the ANOVOR 23 two and three way analysis of variance (Veldman, 1971, p. 246) at the facilities of the computer center at the University of California, Santa Barbara. Correlational analysis was utilized to measure correlation between number of sessions attended and post-treatment GAS scores. Chi-square analyses were computed when appropriate.

Question One

The first experimental question stated: "What are the ethnic, socio-economic, and personal characteristics of Mexican American women who volunteer for the special counseling services of the study?" Considerable variety was found in the areas of appearance, number of children living and dead, and birth place, as well as in those of educational, occupational and economic attainment. During the intake interview, the investigator made gross judgments about the subjects' skin coloring, their style of make-up, their hair grooming and dress. Rated on a scale of one to nine, the subjects were found to be fairly well distributed in the middle part of this continuum (Table 16).

Physical data. Reported age ranged from 20 to 61 years, with fairly even distributions for the categories of 20 - 30, 31 - 40, 41 - 50, and 51 to 61 years (cf: Table 17). A slightly higher percentage (58) was in the 20 - 40 range as compared to 42 percent in the 41 - 61 category. Weight differences ranged from 80 to 220 pounds. The 80 - 120, 121-140, and 141 - 180 pound categories were fairly evenly distributed (cf: Table 18). However, 44 percent whose weight fell within the 141 - 220 pound range were judged to be obese. Height varied from 4'9" to 5'8", with most (69.4 percent) in the 5'1" - 5'4" range (Table 19).

Marital status. The majority of the subjects (94 percent) had been or were married, of these twenty-five percent were in the divorced-separated category, while 13.9 percent were widowed. Eight percent reported never having been married (cf: Table 20). With the exception of one client, the subjects in the divorced-separated category were separated rather than formally divorced. Their separations ranged from one to eleven years in length. Of those married, 69.4 percent had been married once, 19.4 percent twice, and 2.8 percent three times (Table 21).

Number of children. The number of children born to the subjects ranged from zero to fifteen. Because of the high child mortality generally attributed to the poor, the subjects were surveyed not only as to the number of children currently living but also as to the number of children who had died (Table 22). When asked the number of their children currently living, 50 percent reported having four to six children, 22.2 percent reported seven to eight, 19.5 percent reported one to three and 8.3 percent reported having no children living. When asked the number of their children who had died, 75 percent reported having no children who had died, 16.7 percent reported one to three, 5.6 percent reported four to six, and 2.8 percent reported seven to ten children who had died. Thus, twenty-five percent of the subjects reported losing one to ten children by death (cf: Table 22).

TABLE 16

The Subjects' Personal Appearance - Gross Observations Made by the Investigator During the Intake Interview

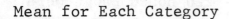

Mean for Each Category

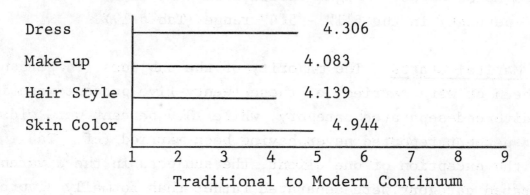

Dress	4.306
Make-up	4.083
Hair Style	4.139
Skin Color	4.944

1   2   3   4   5   6   7   8   9

Traditional to Modern Continuum

TABLE 17

Age Distribution of Clients

Age of Client

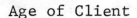

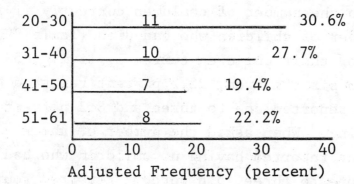

20-30	11	30.6%
31-40	10	27.7%
41-50	7	19.4%
51-61	8	22.2%

0   10   20   30   40

Adjusted Frequency (percent)

TABLE 18

Weight Distribution of Clients

Weight of Client

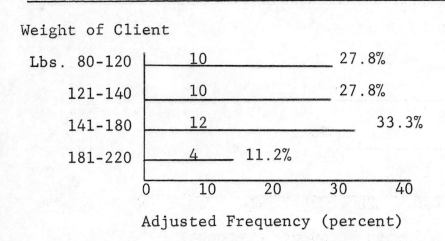

Lbs. 80-120	10	27.8%
121-140	10	27.8%
141-180	12	33.3%
181-220	4	11.2%

Adjusted Frequency (percent)

TABLE 19

Height Distribution of Clients

Height of Clients

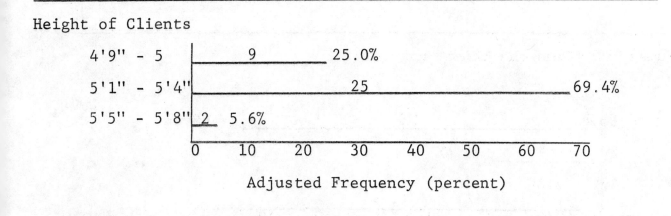

4'9" - 5	9	25.0%
5'1" - 5'4"	25	69.4%
5'5" - 5'8"	2	5.6%

Adjusted Frequency (percent)

TABLE 20

Marital Status Distribution of Clients

Marital Status of Client

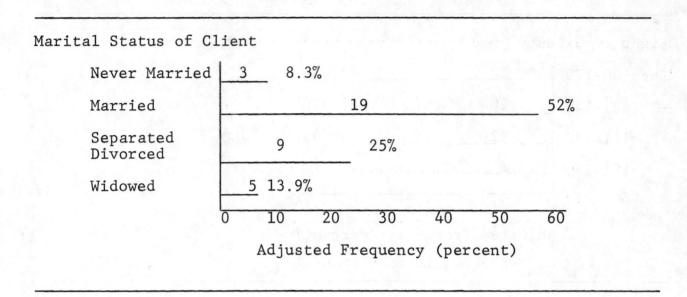

Adjusted Frequency (percent)

TABLE 21

Marital Frequency Distribution of Clients

Number of times the client married

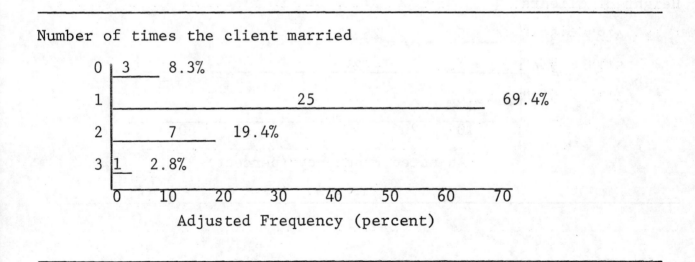

Adjusted Frequency (percent)

TABLE 22

Distribution of Children, Alive and Dead

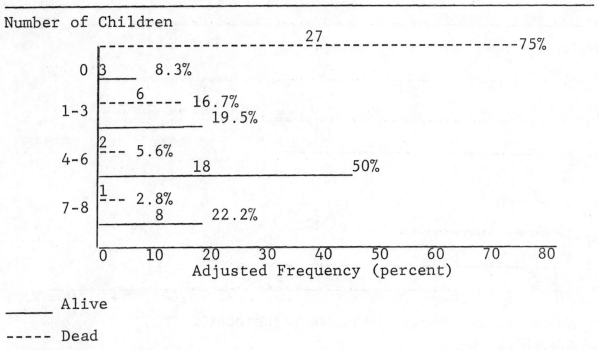

Number of Children

Adjusted Frequency (percent)

_____ Alive

----- Dead

Nativity and Language. Fifty percent of the subjects reported
having been born in Mexico, while the other fifty percent reported
having been born within the United States (cf: Table 23). When
the clients were asked where their first husbands and fathers were
born, only 13.9 percent of their fathers and 35.5 percent of their
husbands were found to have been born in the United States (cf:
Table 23). Thus, the clients were found to have been more frequently born in the United States than were their husbands and
fathers. However, even through fifty percent of the subjects
reported having been born in the United States, only 13.9 percent
reported speaking either only English or primarily English in
their homes (cf: Table 24). Only 27.8 percent reported speaking
both English and Spanish, while 58.3 percent reported speaking only
Spanish or primarily Spanish in the homes.

TABLE 23

Birthplace Distribution of the Clients,
Their Fathers and Husbands

Birthplace

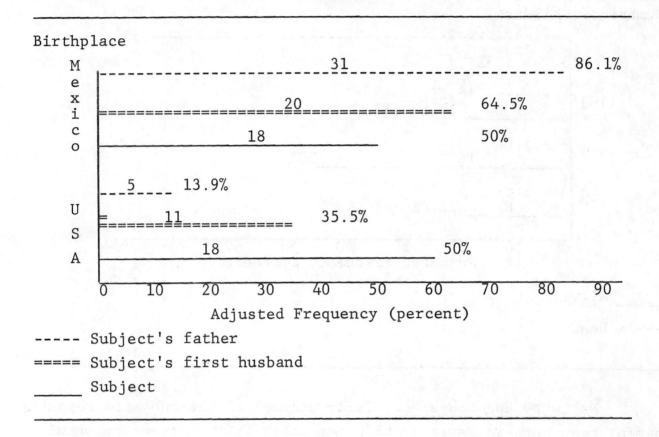

Adjusted Frequency (percent)

----- Subject's father

===== Subject's first husband

_____ Subject

TABLE 24

Distribution of Language the Clients Speak at Home

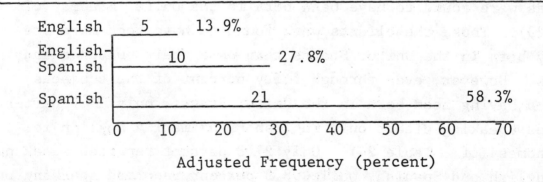

Adjusted Frequency (percent)

Educational, Vocational, and Economic Attainment. The clients reported very low levels of educational attainment in terms of number of school grades completed. Low scholastic attainment was also reported for their fathers and their husbands (cf: Table 25). A total of 63.3 percent of the subjects reported having zero to six grades of schooling, and 63.6 percent of their fathers and 52.7 percent of their husbands had also attained this same low educational level. Only 8.3 percent of the subjects, 6.3 percent of their husbands, and 3.8 percent of their fathers finished high school.

Additionally, their occupational attainment and that of their husbands and fathers was also quite low (Table 26); 86.1 percent of the clients, 64.6 percent of their husbands and 68.8 percent of their fathers were in the semi-skilled category. Specific occupations reported under these general categories are presented in Table 27.

Consistent with the subjects' very low education-vocational levels, was a report of low economic attainment. Their reported gross annual income per person for each family ranged from zero to $2,000 (Table 28). Many of the subjects were receiving welfare, social security or other monetary assistance which was included in their reported income. The one individual who reported no income was not working because of cancer, was separated from her husband and could not receive welfare assistance because she was in the United States illegally. The annual income of fifty percent of the subjects was in the zero to $750 per person per year category, while the other fifty percent reported annual incomes ranging from $750 to $2,000 per person.

Physical health. In response to the question "How is your health?", 55.6 percent reported that they were in poor health, while 30.6 percent reported fair health and only 13.9 percent reported good or excellent health (Table 29). Fifty-seven percent reported suffering from multiple physical symptoms while only nine percent reported no physical symptoms (Table 30). Since 69.7

TABLE 25

Distribution of Educational Attainment of the Clients,
the Clients' Fathers, and the Clients' Husbands

School Grades Completed

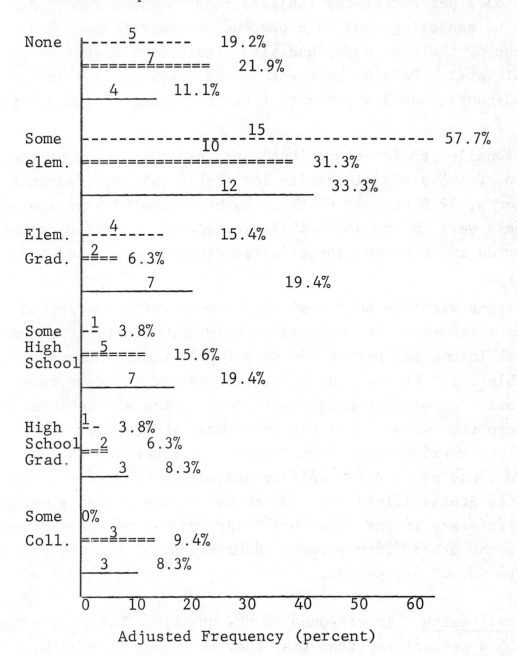

Adjusted Frequency (percent)

-------Subject's father

=======Subject's first husband

_____Subject

TABLE 26

Distribution of Occupational Attainment for the Clients,
the Client's Father and First Husband

Occupational Attainment

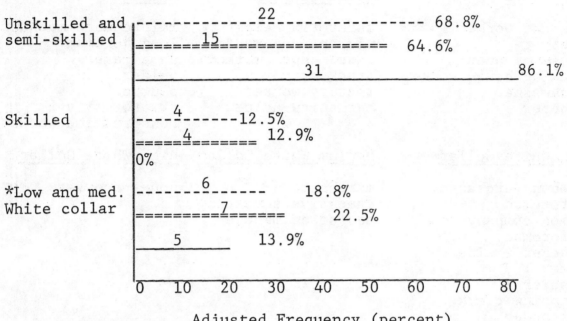

Adjusted Frequency (percent)

----- Subject's father

===== Subject's first husband

_____ Subject

* For specific reported occupations under these general categories
see Table 27.

TABLE 27

Reported Occupations of the Clients, Their Fathers, and Their
Husbands Under General Categories

Unskilled	Semi-Skilled	Skilled
migrant worker	cafeteria helper	maintenance mechanic
janitor	migrant contractor	longshoreman
house cleaner	water dept. worker	shoe maker
packing house worker	truck driver	welder
dishwasher	factory worker	plumber
laborer	mechanics helper	tractor driver
		construction worker

Low White Collar	Medium White Collar	High White Collar
lumber yard asst. foreman	merchant	none reported
lemon company asst. foreman	executive secretary	
teacher's aide	assistant manager	
baker		
cashier		
shipping clerk		
bartender		

TABLE 28

Distribution of the Clients' Reported Gross
Annual Income Per Person

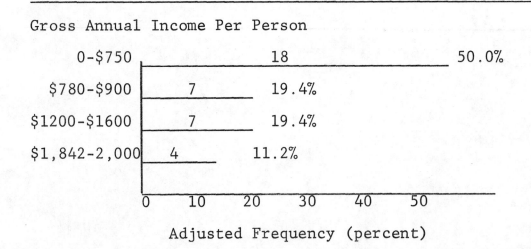

Gross Annual Income Per Person

0-$750	18	50.0%
$780-$900	7	19.4%
$1200-$1600	7	19.4%
$1,842-2,000	4	11.2%

0   10   20   30   40   50

Adjusted Frequency (percent)

TABLE 29

Distribution of the Clients' Health Opinion

Clients' Health Opinion

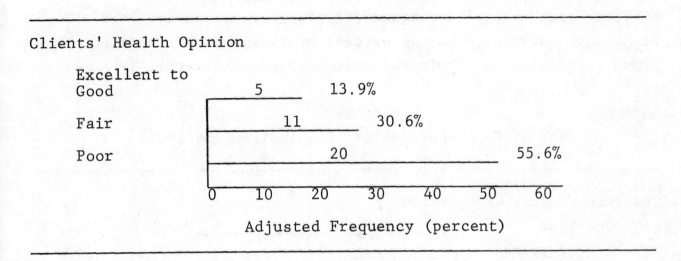

Adjusted Frequency (percent)

Clients' Health Opinion		
Excellent to Good	5	13.9%
Fair	11	30.6%
Poor	20	55.6%

TABLE 30

Distribution of Physical Symptoms Reported by the Clients

Physical Symptoms Reported by the Clients

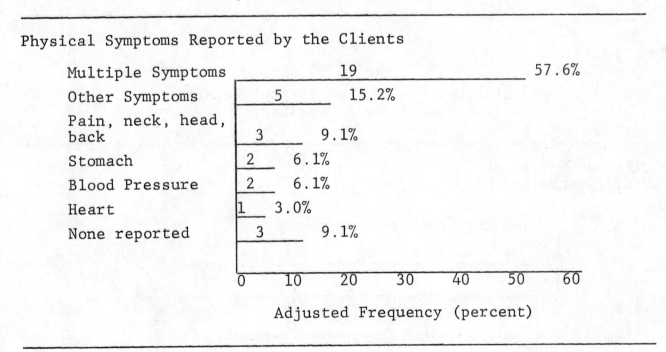

Adjusted Frequency (percent)

Physical Symptoms Reported by the Clients		
Multiple Symptoms	19	57.6%
Other Symptoms	5	15.2%
Pain, neck, head, back	3	9.1%
Stomach	2	6.1%
Blood Pressure	2	6.1%
Heart	1	3.0%
None reported	3	9.1%

percent reported having had a complete physical examination within one year, 15.2 percent within one to two years and 15.2 percent within two or more years (Table 31), it is apparent that the subjects seek medical assistance for their reported low levels of health. However, only 36 percent of the subjects reported prior counseling for their psychological problems (cf: Table 32).

TABLE 31

Date of Complete Physical Examination (Medical)

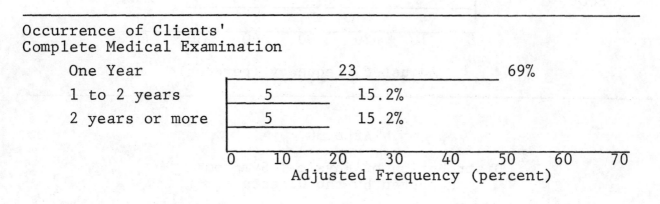

Occurrence of Clients'
Complete Medical Examination

One Year	23	69%
1 to 2 years	5	15.2%
2 years or more	5	15.2%

Adjusted Frequency (percent)

TABLE 32

Distribution of the Clients' Reports
of Prior Counseling

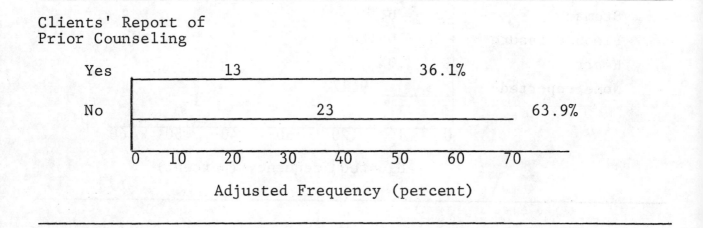

Clients' Report of
Prior Counseling

Yes	13	36.1%
No	23	63.9%

Adjusted Frequency (percent)

Question Two

Question two asked: "What problem categories are most frequently presented during the intake interview?" To answer this question, the subjects were interviewed as to their need for other services, with 52 - 94.4 percent indicating a need for financial, medical, legal, vocation, educational, and marital and/or family counseling services (cf: Table 33). The most frequently reported need (94.4 percent) was for marital and/or family counseling services, while 83.3 percent reported the need for job training, 58.3 percent for financial assistance, 52.8 percent for legal aide, 58.3 percent for medical service and 52.8 percent reported needing English classes.

Additionally, the multiple target complaints presented at the intake interview by the clients were ranked according to frequency of occurrence (cf: Table 34 and Table 35). Most frequently cited were depression, low self esteem, decision making problems, and disharmony with husband or lover, i.e., with a male with whom the subject was cohabitating. Even though depression was one of the most frequent reported problem areas (80.6), it was not followed by a high incidence of suicide history and/or reported current serious attempts or plans to end life. Depression areas reported were frequently associated with chronic and severe marital disharmony as well as with the death of a family member, poor physical health and financial problems. Marital disharmony was frequently associated with reported physical aggression from the husband. Twenty-five percent of the married clients reported aggression, while 22.2 did not; 8.3 percent of the women in the separated-divorced category reported agression while 22.2 percent did not; 11.1 percent of the clients in the widowed category reported aggression as compared to 2.8 percent who did not (cf: Table 36).

Question Three

Question three stated: "To what problem areas do low socio-economic Mexican American women address themselves most frequently during counseling sessions?" In order to answer this question, a

TABLE 33

Distribution of the Clients' Reported Needs
for Auxilliary Services

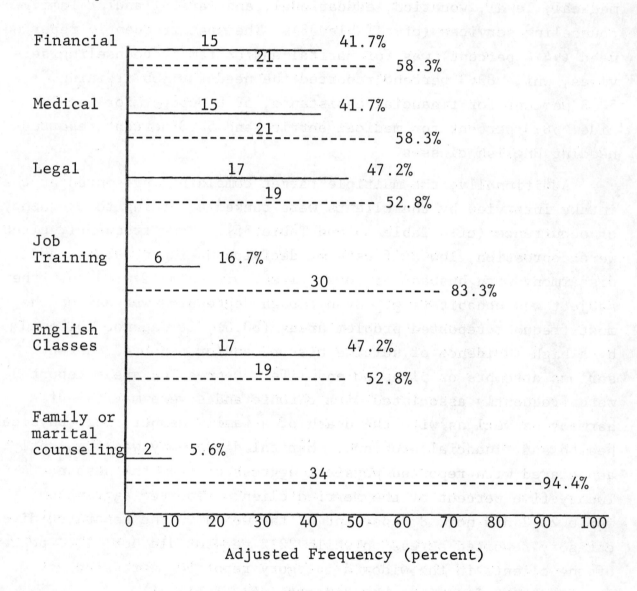

Services Requested

Financial	15	41.7%
	21	58.3%
Medical	15	41.7%
	21	58.3%
Legal	17	47.2%
	19	52.8%
Job Training	6	16.7%
	30	83.3%
English Classes	17	47.2%
	19	52.8%
Family or marital counseling	2	5.6%
	34	94.4%

Adjusted Frequency (percent)

------- Yes

_____ No

TABLE 34

Distribution of Target Complaints Most Frequently Presented at the Intake Interview (GAS)

Rank	Target Complaint	Adjusted Frequency (Percent)	
1.	Depression	30	80.6%
2.	Low Self Esteem	30	77.8%
3.	Decision Making Problems	24	64.7%
4.	Disharmony-Husband or Lover	23	62.9%
5.	Problem Related to Poor English Fluency	21	58.3%
6.	Dependency	20	57.1%
7.	Inappropriate Affect	18	50.0%
8.	Problem Related to Lack of Diversion	17	42.4%
9.	Disharmony - Children	15	40%
10.	Anxiety Symptoms	15	36.4%
11.	Agression-from Family	14	26.7%
12.	Problems Related to Financial Needs	14	26.7%
13.	Somatic Problems	10	23.5%

0 10 20 30 40 50 60 70 80

TABLE 35

Distribution of Target Complaints Least Frequently Presented
at the Intake Interview (GAS)

Rank	Target Complaint	Adjusted Frequency (Percent)	
1	Drug Abuse - Self	1	2.8%
2	Problems Related to Religion	1	2.8%
3	Alcohol Abuse - Self	2	5.6%
4	Disharmony with Family (Parents or Siblings)	4	5.9%
5	Psychotic History and/or Current Symptoms	5	6.1%
6	Drug Abuse - Family	3	8.3%
7	Alcohol Abuse - Family	3	10%
8	Problems Related to Death of Family Member	4	11.8%
9	Agression Toward Family	5	13.9%
10	Current Family Planning Problems	5	14.3%
11	Psychosis History and/or Current Symptoms-Family	5	14.3%
12	Problems Related to Legal Difficulties	5	18.5%
13	Suicide History and/or Symptoms	7	19.4%
14	Sexual Problems	7	20%

0   10   20   30

TABLE 36

Distribution of the Subjects' Reported Physical Aggressions
by the Husband or Lover

Reported Aggression According to Marital Status

Married
    _____8_____ 22.2%
    ------9------ 25.0%

Separated
Divorced
    _____8_____ 22.2%
    ---3--- 8.3%

Widowed
    _1_ 2.8%
    ---4--- 11.1%

Single
    _3_ 8.4%

    0   10   20   30   40
    Adjusted Frequency (percent)

----- Aggression

_____ No Aggression

content analysis was made of the counselors' summary notes for
each session. Problem areas discussed by the clients and summarized by the counselors were identified, described, and labeled
under broad problem categories (cf: Table 37). Problem areas
most frequently discussed in each counseling session were identified by determining the percentage of clients who had discussed
the problem (cf: Table 38). Problems related to disharmony with
husband or lover and with the subjects' children were most frequently discussed.

TABLE 37

Problem Areas Discussed by the Subjects as Recorded in the Counselors' Summaries

I. Relationship problems
   A. With husband or lover
   B. With parents or siblings
   C. With others
   D. With agencies

II. External Problems or Needs
   A. Medical problems
   B. Religious problems
   C. Legal Problems
   D. Sexual problems
   E. Occupational problems
   F. Diversional needs
   G. Financial needs
   H. Alcohol or drug problems
   I. Prejudicial problems
   J. Problems related to mourning of dead family members

III. Internal Problems or Symptoms
   A. Low self esteem
   B. Anxiety symptoms
   C. Depression symptoms
   D. Psychotic symptoms

IV. Reported Improvement and/or "Happy Talk"

TABLE 38

Distribution of Most Frequently Discussed Problem Areas
as Recorded in the Counselors' Summaries

Session No.	Problem Area	(Rank	Adjusted Frequency (Percent)	
			Yes	No
I	Relationship to husband	1	68	32
	Relationship to children	2	33	67
	relationship to parents	3	22	78
II	Relationship to husband	1	75	25
	Relationship to children	2	41	59
	Medical problems	3	22	78
III	Relationship to husband	1	48	52
	Relationship to children	2	48	52
	Relationship to others	3	24	76
IV	Relationship to children	1	50	50
	Relationship to husband	2	45	55
	Medical Problems	3	28	62
V	Relationship to children	1	47	53
	Relationship to husband	2	47	53
VI	Relationship to husband	1	54	46
	Relationship to others	2	31	69
	Relationship to children	3	30	70
	Reported improvement	4	29	71
VII	Relationship to husband	1	53.8	46.2
	Relationship to children	2	38.5	61.5
	Medical problems	3	30	70
VIII	Relationship to children	1	43	57
	Relationship to husband	2	24	76

Question Four

Question four stated: "Which type of referral sources are most effective in motivating low socio-economic Mexican American women to seek counseling?" To answer this question, several methods were employed over a period of four months to recruit the subjects. These methods are described in Chapter II. The results of these efforts yielded 43 telephone calls by individual Mexican American women requesting an appointment with the investigator. Of these 43 appointments, only 36 (83.7 percent) kept their appointments. Of these 36 subjects, 42.2 percent reported that they were referred by an agency such as Mental Health, who alone referred 22.2 percent, 16.7 percent stated that a community person had referred them, 17.7 percent said they were prompted to call by the radio and newspaper announcements, while 19.4 percent reported that they came because they received personal letters (Table 39). Letters distributed as leaflets to private residences did not yield any subjects, nor agencies such as Probation, public schools or Head Start.

TABLE 39

Distribution of Clients' Referral Sources

Method of Referral

Letter	7	19.4%
Radio-News Paper	6	16.7%
Agency	17	42.2%
Community Person	6	16.7%

```
        0       10       20       30       40       50
```

Adjusted Frequency (percent)

Question Five

Question five stated: "How important is the provision of auxilliary services, e.g., transportation and baby-sitting, to this population seeking and continuing in counseling?" Even though baby-sitting and transportation were available to all the subjects only a small number utilized these services (Table 40). A majority of the subjects (72.2 percent) did not use the available transportation (Table 40), primarily because most of them (66.7 percent) came from neighborhoods of Oxnard near the setting of the study and thus did not need transportation. Only 11.1 percent came from Ventura and 22.2 percent from the nearby cities of Saticoy, Santa Paula, Port Hueneme and Camaraillo (Table 41). Thus, 33.3 percent came from cities other than Oxnard and 27.8 percent utilized the transportation services. Utilization of the available baby-sitting services was also low (16.7 percent), and may be explained by the fact that all counseling was conducted on Saturday so that the subjects were able to leave their young children in the care of older children who were free to baby-sit.

Research questions one through five can be summarized by describing a typical client of this study: Mrs. Sanchez's skin coloring is light to medium olive. Her dress, make-up and hair style fails to reflect a very traditional or modern appearance. Her height ranges between 5'1" to 5'4" and her weight is between 141 to 180 pounds. She is married, and has four to six children living. She states that she prefers Spanish during the counseling sessions and that in the home she speaks Spanish only or Spanish primarily. The Spanish she uses is correct, formal and polite. She has completed six grades or less of school and is a housewife who also works part time in the fields, in the packing houses, or in someone's home as a maid. Her income is very low ($750 or less per year). She states that she is in poor health and complains of multiple symptoms (high bloof pressure, diabetes and chronic headaches). She reports many needs for auxilliary services, e.g., special family and/or marital counseling. She is afraid that her daughter is mentally ill because of her bizarre

TABLE 40

Distribution of the Clients' Use of the Baby-sitting and Transporation Services

Clients' Use of Baby-sitting and Transportation

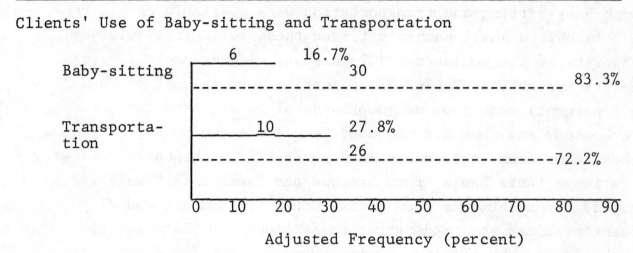

Adjusted Frequency (percent)

_____ Yes

------ No

TABLE 41

Distribution of the Clients' City of Residence

Cities Where the Clients Reside

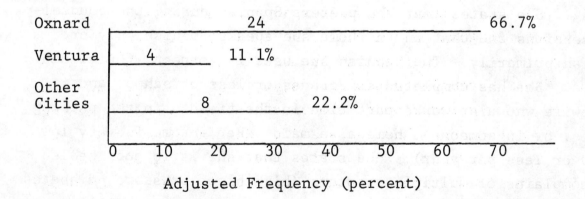

Adjusted Frequency (percent)

behavior and is concerned because her son has been unable to get a job. Her main worry is her alcoholic husband who has frequently swollen her face and bruised her body with his physical aggression, and who has failed to provide her and the children with needed support. She expresses much ambivalence concerning what she wishes to do about her husband. She cries when she describes her husband's beatings. She expresses low self-esteem and self-anger as she states that she is nothing but a pendeja (fool). Even though she looks very depressed she denies suicide history or current plans to end life. She does not require baby-sitting or transportation because she lives a few blocks from the counseling setting. She expresses much appreciation of the investigators' attention and agrees to return for counseling with her assigned counselor.

Testing the Study's Hypotheses

In addition to answering the above five research questions, this study proposed and tested four hypotheses which utilized therapeutic change and treatment attendance as dependent variables, and which tested the relationship of therapeutic outcomes to treatment attendance. Additionally, a 50:50 null hypothesis of the subject's language preference during counseling was tested. Descriptive primary data collected by pre- and post-assessments with the Goal Attainment Scale was used as the criteria for appraising therapeutic outcomes. Attendance at treatment was used as an additional criteria for evaluating treatment effectiveness as recommended by Krebs (1971).

Hypothesis 1. Hypothesis 1 stated: "Subjects exposed to Behavior Rehearsal will demonstrate more favorable therapeutic outcomes as measured by post-assessment on the Goal Attainment Scale than will subjects exposed to Therapeutic Listening." To test this hypothesis, analysis of variance for disproportionate subclass frequencies was utilized with the pre-test and post-test scores of each of the five scales of the Goal Attainment Scale (Table 42 and Table 43). These scales referred to five problem areas

67

TABLE 42

Analysis of Variance Based Upon Pre-test Scores of each GAS Scale-Treatment Condition and Counselor as main effects

SCALE ONE

Variation Source	M.S.	D.F.	F.Ratio	P
Total	0.411	26		
Between	0.186	5		
A(Counselor)	0.006	2	0.0120	0.9890
B(Treatment)	0.002	1	0.0040	0.9489
AB(Interaction)	0.007	2		
Within	0.464	21		

Means for all Effects:

	1	2	3
A(Counselor)	-1.2000	-1.2500	-1.2250

	1	2
B(Treatment)	-1.2333	-1.2167

Means for Counselor-Treatment Effects

Counselor	Behavior Rehearsal 1	Therapeutic Listening 2
1	-1.0000	-1.4000
2	-1.5000	-1.0000
3	-1.2000	-1.2500

SCALE TWO

Variation Source	M.S.	D.F.	F. Ratio	P
Total	0.252	26		
Between	0.220	5		
A(Counselor)	0.496	2	1.9124	0.1712
B(Treatment)	0.002	1	0.0071	0.9315
AB(Interaction)	0.052	2	0.1998	0.8218
Within	0.260	21		

Means for all Effects:

	1	2	3
A(Counselor	-1.6750	-1.3250	-1.2250
B(Treatment)	-1.4000	-1.4167	

	Means for Counselor-Treatment Effects	
	Behavior Rehearsal	Therapeutic Listening
Counselor	1	2
1	-1.7500	-1.6000
2	- .2500	-1.4000
3	-1.200	-1.2500

Variation Source	M.S	D.F.	F. Ratio	P
Total	0.238	26		
Between	0.239	5		
A(Counselor)	0.207	1	0.8711	0.5639
B(Treatment)	0.067	2	0.2800	0.6080
AB(Interaction)	0.356		1.4933	0.2467
Within	0.238	21		

Means for all Effects:

	1	2	3
A(Counselor	-1.4500	-1.6500	-1.7500
B(Treatment)	-1.6667	-1.5667	

Means for Counselor-Treatment Effects

Counselor	Behavior Rehearsal 1	Therapeutic Listening 2
1	-1.5000	-1.4000
2	-1.5000	-1.8000
3	-2.000	-1.5000

SCALE FOUR

Variation Source	M.S.	D.F.	F. Ratio	P
Total	0.409	26		
Between	0.084	5		
A(Counselor)	0.089	2	0.1830	0.8351
B(Treatment)	0.185	1	0.3812	0.5501
AB(Interaction)	0.030	2	0.0610	0.9407
Within	0.486	21		

Means for all Effects:

	1	2	3
A(Counselor)	-1.550	-1.6500	-1.4500
B(Treatment)	-1.4667	-1.6333	

Means for Counselor-Treatment Effects

Counselor	Behavior Rehearsal 1	Therapeutic Listening 2
1	-1.5000	-1.6000
2	-1.5000	-1.8000
3	-1.400	-1.5000

SCALE FIVE

Variation Source	M.S.	D.F.	F. RATIO	P
Total	0.241	26		
Between	0.114	5		
A(Counselor)	0.135	2	0.4981	0.6198
B(Treatment)	0.118	1	0.4365	0.5225
AB(Interaction)	0.091	2	0.3343	0.7239
Within	0.271	21		

Means for all Effects:

	1	2	3
A(Counselor)	-1.7750	-1.5750	-1.5500
B(Treatment)	-1.7000	-1.5667	

	Means for Counselor-Treatment Effects	
	Behavior Rehearsal	Therapeutic Listening
Counselor	1	2
1	-1.7500	-1.8000
2	-1.7500	-1.4000
3	-1.6000	-1.5000

TABLE 43

Analysis of Variance Based Upon Post-Test Scores of each Scale of the GAS - Treatment Condition and Counselor as Main Effects

SCALE ONE

Variation Source	M.S.	D.F.	F. Ratio	P
Total	1.870	26		
Between	3.354	5		
A(Counselor)	1.422	2	0.9377	0.5903
B(Treatment)	2.535	1	1.6715	0.2079
AB(Interaction)	5.696	2	3.7558	0.0393*
Within	1.517	21	* = $p < .05$	

Means for all Effects:

	1	2	3
A(Counselor)	-0.2750	0.1250	0.5250
B(Treatment)	0.4333	-0.1833	

Counselor	Means for Counselor-Treatment Effects	
	Behavior Rehearsal 1	Therapeutic Listening 2
1	-0.7500	0.2000
2	1.2500	-1.0000
3	0.8000	0.2500

SCALE TWO

Variation Source	M.S.	D.F.	F. Ratio	P
Total	2.172	26		
Between	3.866	5		
A(Counselor)	1.239	2	0.7003	0.5117
B(Treatment)	14.669	1	8.2918	0.0088*
AB(Interaction)	1.091	2	0.6166	0.5538
Within	1.769	21		* = $p < .01$

Means for all Effects

	1	2	3
A(Counselor)	-0.1000	0.6000	0.4750
B(Treatment)	1.0667	-0.4167	

	Means for Counselor-Treatment Effects	
	Behavior Rehearsal	Therapeutic Listening
Counselor	1	2
1	1.0000	-1.2000
2	1.0000	0.2000
3	1.2000	-0.2500

SCALE THREE

Variation Source	M.S.	D.F.	F. Ratio	P
Total	1.580	26		
Between	1.234	5		
A(Treatment)	2.757	2	1.6592	0.2131
B(Counselor)	0.474	1	0.2853	0.6047
AB(Interaction)	0.091	2	0.0546	0.9469
Within	1.662	21		

Means for all Effects:

	1	2	3
A(Counselor)	0.6750	-0.3250	-0.2500
B(Treatment)	0.1667	-0.1000	

	Means for Counselor-Treatment Effects	
	Behavior Rehearsal	Therapeutic Listening
Counselor	1	2
1	0.7500	0.6000
2	-0.2500	-0.4000
3	0.0	-0.5000

SCALE FOUR

Variation Source	M.S.	D.F.	F Ratio	P
Total	1.537	26		
Between	1.282	5		
A(Counselor)	1.980	2	1.2391	0.3101
B(Treatment)	0.980	1	0.6132	0.5519
AB(Interaction)	0.735	2	0.4602	0.6426
Within	1.598	21		

Means for all Effects:

	1	2	3
A(Counselor)	-1.2000	-0.9000	-0.2750
B(Treatment	-0.6000	-0.9833	

	Means for Counselor-Treatment Effects	
	Behavior Rehearsal	Therapeutic Listening
Counselor	1	2
1	-1.0000	-1.4000
2	-1.0000	-0.8000
3	0.2000	-0.7500

76

SCALE FIVE

Variation Source	M.S.	D.F.	F Ratio	P
Total	1.849	26		
Between	1.504	5		
A(Counselor)	1.146	2	0.5936	0.5659
B(Treatment)	0.535	1	0.2772	0.6098
AB (Interaction)	2.346	2	1.3151	0.3169
Within	1.931	21		

Means for all Effects:

	1	2	3
A(Counselor)	-0.7250	-0.0500	-0.6000
B(Treatment)	-0.3167	-0.6000	

	Means for Counselor-Treatment Effects	
	Behavior Rehearsal	Therapeutic Listening
Counselor	1	2
1	-0.2500	-1.2000
2	-0.5000	0.4000
3	-0.2000	-1.0000

specific to each client on which five possible levels of treatment
attainment, from most unfavorable (given -2 value) to most favorable
(given +2 value), had been specified. On the basis of this analysis for the pre-test, subjects assigned to Therapeutic Listening
Treatment model did not differ significantly from those assigned
to Behavior Rehearsal on any of the GAS categories. The analysis of variance for disproportionate sub-class frequencies on
the post-test scores provides the data from which the hypothesis
was tested. To test this hypothesis each scale was analyzed
individually (cf: Table 43). Only for scale two, which represents the problem area second most important to the client, were
differences reaching traditional levels of significance found.
Specific problem areas recorded in sale two are presented in
Appendix G. On this scale subjects exposed to Behavioral Rehearsal did show a significant increase in favorable treatment
outcomes as measured by the GAS (p .008). Thus, on the basis
of this data we would reject the null hypothesis and conclude that
this difference would occur by chance less than eight times out
of one thousand. Significant differences were not found for
scales one, three, four, and five. However, the means were in
the direction hypothesized. In addition, a significant counselor-
treatment interaction was found for scale one. This interaction
indicates that while one counselor (counselor three) appears
equally effective with both treatments, counselor one was more
effective with Therapeutic Listening and counselor two was more
effective with Behavior Rehearsal.

Hypothesis 2. Hypothesis 2 stated: "Subjects exposed to
behavior Rehearsal will attend counseling sessions more frequently than will subjects exposed to Therapeutic Listening."
Of the initial 36 clients who were pre-tested at the intake
interview and randomly assigned to the treatment conditions
(Table 44), only 28 came to one or more counseling sessions
(Table 45). The reasons given by the eight subjects for failing
to attend counseling are presented in Table 46. Fifty percent of

TABLE 44

Distribution of Subjects Random Assignment to
Treatment and Counselor Conditions

| Counselor | Treatment Model | |
	Behavior Rehearsal	Therapeutic Listening
1	6	6
2	6	6
3	6	6

$$N = 36$$

TABLE 45

Distribution of Subjects Attending One or More Counseling
Sessions According to Counselor and Treatment

| Counselor | Treatment | |
	Behavior Rehearsal	Therapeutic Listening
1	6	4
2	4	5
3	4	5

$$N_1 + N_2 = N \ 28$$

79

TABLE 46

Reasons given by the Subjects who Failed to
Attend any Counseling Sessions

Subject Number	Reason for Not Attending Counseling
1	Stated she would only accept the investigator as her counselor
10, 29	Both stated that they now knew the source of their problems and further counseling was not needed
13	Stated she wanted a psychiatrist as her therapist. Refused to accept assignment to a counselor
26	Stated husband threatened her with physical violence if she attended counseling
29	Found a job which interfered with the time for counseling
32	Moved out of town to escape husband's "cruel behavior"

the subjects attended four to eight sessions, while 27.8 percent attended one to three sessions and 22.2 percent attended only the intake interview (Table 47). Treatment attendance according to treatment model (Table 48) was computed and the mean number of sessions attended by the subjects assigned to each treatment was found to be 5.177 for Behavior Rehearsal and 5.150 for Therapeutic Listening (Table 49). Because inspection of these two means indicated that they were too close to be significantly different, further analysis to test significant differences was not done.

Based on these results, the null hypothesis was not rejected, and we would conclude that subjects exposed to Behavior Rehearsal did not differ significantly from subjects exposed to Therapeutic

TABLE 47

Distribution of the Clients Treatment Attendance

Clients Treatment Attendance

Intake only	8	22.2%
1-3 Sessions	10	27.8%
4-8 Sessions	18	50%

```
    0    10    20    30    40    50    60
```

Adjusted Frequency (Percent)

TABLE 48

Distribution of Levels of Attendance at Counseling
for the Two Treatment Conditions

Treatment Attendance	Treatment Assignment		Total
	Behavior Rehearsal	Therapeutic Listening	
Intake only	4	4	8
1 to 6 sessions	8	7	15
7 to 8 sessions	6	7	13

TABLE 49

Mean Treatment Attendance as Related to
Counselor and Treatment Model

| | Treatment Model | |
Counselor	Behavior Rehearsal	Therapeutic Listening
1	3.25	5.60
2	6.25	3.60
3	6.00	6.25
Total	15.50	15.45
Mean	5.166	5.150

TABLE 50

Perason Correlation Coefficient Results Testing the
Relationship of Treatment Attendance to Treatment Outcome as
Measured by the Post-Treatment GAS Scores

Post-Treatment Goal Attainment Scale	r	P
Scale 1	.21	Not Significant
Scale 2	-.11	Not Significant
Scale 3	.01	Not Significant
Scale 4	-.11	Not Significant
Scale 5	.09	Not Significant

Listening in respect to attendance rates.

Hypothesis 3. Hypothesis 3 stated: "The relationship between treatment attendance and therapeutic outcome will be positive." To gain an answer to this question a Pearson correlation coefficient was utilized to measure the relationship between attendance rates and post-assessment scores on the GAS summed over all five scales. The correlation coefficient between these two variables for all subjects was -.15; for Behavior Rehearsal it was +.16, and for Therapeutic Listening -.24. This same correlation analysis was done with each scale of the GAS and the results were not significant (Table 50).

Hypothesis 4. Hypothesis 4 stated: "The subjects will more frequently prefer to speak Spanish than English during the counseling sessions." Sixty-four percent of the subjects were found to prefer to speak Spanish during counseling, while 22.2 percent preferred English, and 13.9 percent preferred a mixture of English and Spanish (Table 51). A chi-square analysis was used to test the 50:50 null hypothesis which stated that 50 percent of the subjects would prefer to speak English, while 50 percent of the subjects would prefer to speak Spanish. This analysis was based on 31 subjects; those five subjects who preferred the English - Spanish mixture were not considered. Based on this analysis the null hypothesis was rejected at the .01 level of significance and we would conclude that the subjects would more frequently prefer Spanish to English during counseling.

TABLE 51

Distribution of the Subjects' Reported Language
Preference During Counseling

_____

Language Preference Counseling

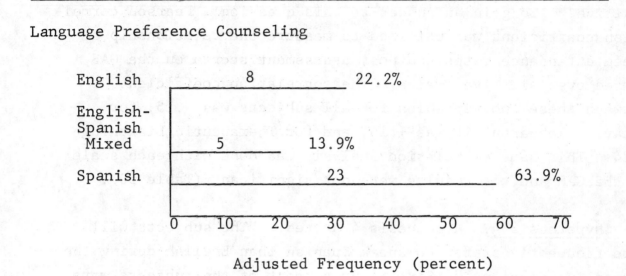

Adjusted Frequency (percent)

_____

CHAPTER IV

SUMMARY AND CONCLUSIONS

Summary of the Study

This investigation was designed to compare and test experimentally the therapeutic effectiveness of two individual counseling strategies, Therapeutic Listening and Behavior Rehearsal, with low income Mexican American women. More specifically, this study sought to determine which of these two counseling procedures was more effective in promoting attainment of five client specific goals which were elicited, labeled, ranked and scaled according to the specifications of the Goal Attainment Scale (Appendix E). Attendance in therapy was used as an additional dependent variable.

Four hypotheses were tested. It was hypothesized that exposure to Behavior Rehearsal would significantly effect more favorable therapeutic outcomes in terms of client-specific goals and more frequent attendance at treatment. It was further hypothesized that treatment attendance would be positively correlated to therapeutic outcomes. In addition, it was predicted that Spanish would be the language more frequently preferred in counseling than English.

The study also sought answers to the following research questions: (1) "What are the ethnic, socio-economic and personal characteristics of Mexican American women who volunteered for the special counseling services of the study?" (2) "What problem categories are most frequently presented during the initial intake interview?" (3) "To what problem areas do low socio-economic Mexican American women address themselves most frequently during counseling sessions?" (4) "Which type of referral sources are most effective in motivating low socio-economic Mexican American women to seek counseling?" (5) "How important is the provision of auxiliary services, e.g., transportation and baby-sitting, to this population's seeking and continuing in counseling?"

The investigation was conducted in a community owned and operated multiple service center of Oxnard, California. The 36 subjects were low income Mexican American women residing in Ventura County, California, who volunteered for counseling services. Randomization procedures were used for assigning all subjects to one of two treatment conditions for eight weekly counseling sessions of 45 minutes each and to one of three counselors. The subjects' language preference was used during the counseling sessions as well as during the intake interview. The counselors selected for this study were bilingual, female, college graduates of 30 years of age or over. Specific procedures were utilized to train the counselors in the two treatment conditions of the study: Behavior Rehearsal, a relatively new behavioral counseling model which combines role playing and social modeling, and Therapeutic Listening, a variant of Roger's client-centered therapy which utilizes the therapeutic mechanisms of insight and catharsis.

To insure that the treatment conditions had not been violated, all counseling sessions were tape recorded when the client gave her permission. The first 30 minutes of two tapes for each counselor in both treatment conditions were randomly selected and rated by two bilingual counselors-in-training who utilized a specific rating scale designed for this purpose (see Appendix F). High inter-judge reliability for these two raters were found for each of the five sections of the Rating Scale (r_1 = .66, r_2 = .85, r_3 = 1, r_4 = 1, r_5 = 1).

A pre-test post-test group design was utilized. Pre-treatment assessment was accomplished during an intake interview with each client who was encouraged to discuss the reasons which led her to seek counseling. From these discussions, five target complaints were first selected and labeled, and then ranked and scaled into five levels of possible treatment outcomes by the investigator who used the Goal Attainment Scale, an instrument developed for this purpose. The five levels of treatment outcomes ranged from least favorable (given a -2 value), to most favorable (given a +2 value). A specific outcome level was selected by the investigator for each of the client's five target complaints. Post-assessments were scheduled eight to ten weeks from the initial intake interview. However, due to multiple complications, such as frequent trips to Mexico and illness in the family, the post-assessment were rescheduled for eight to twelve weeks from pre-assessment. The post-assessments were accomplished by a bilingual, female, interviewer who met with each client individually and utilizing the previously specified GAS, determined the current therapeutic attainment level for each of the subject's target complaints.

Of the 36 subjects accepted for the study, only 28 attended one or more counseling sessions, and of these only 27 were post-tested. One subject moved to Mexico and was unable to be contacted. A 3x2 analysis of variance for disproportionate subclass frequencies was carried out with the type of treatment model and counselor as main effects. Correlational analyses were also utilized to measure the relationship between number of sessions attended and post-treatment outcomes. In addition, a chi-square analysis was used to test a 50:50 null hypothesis of the client's language preference.

Discussion of Results

Data in respect to the five research questions generally: (1) supported comments made by Penalosa (1967, 1970) and Grebler et al., (1970) concerning the heterogeneity of the Mexican Americans; (2) reinforced the disadvantaged demographic profile of the Mexican American (cf: Chapter I); and (3) demonstrated the prevalence of marital disharmony and marital disruptions, e.g., separation and divorce, which the literature (Barrett, 1966; Moore with Cuellar, 1970; Grebler et al, 1970), and this investigator's clinical experience supports.

Personal characteristics. The subjects' skin coloring
ranged from very fair to very dark olive, with the majority having light to medium olive skin. Their dress, make-up and hair
style ranged from very modern to very traditional, e.g., long
braids, no make-up, long modest-looking dresses. Most of the
women were in the middle part of this continuum. Their height
was most frequently in the 5'1"-5'4" range and their weight in
the 141-180 pound range. Most of them (94 percent) had been or
were married and 50 percent had four to six children living.
Even though 50 percent reported having been born in the United
States, only 13.9 percent reported speaking exclusively or
primarily English in their homes.

Educational, occupational, and economic attainment.
Educationally, occupationally, and economically the clients
were found to be more disadvantaged than the general Mexican
American population of the Southwest (cf: Grebler et al, 1970).
The majority (56.6 percent) described their health as poor and
69.7 percent mentioned more than one physical symptom. This
is consistent with the reported low levels of health of the
poor (Mechanic, 1969; Humphrey, 1965). Sixty-nine percent
stated that they had undergone a complete physical examination
within the past year; however, only 36 percent had received
prior counseling even though they reported chronic psychological
problems.

Problem categories. Consistent with the subjects' low
educational, vocational, and economic attainments and their
characteristically large families and poor health levels,
was their reported need for multiple services. Financial,
medical, legal, vocational, educational and marital and/or
family counseling were the requested services, with the majority
(94.4 percent) indicating their need for marital and/or family
counseling. Multiple target complaints or mental health problems
were reported, the most frequent being depression, low self-

esteem, decision making problems and disharmony with husband or lover. Depression was rarely associated with suicide history and/or current serious attempts to end life. Instead, depression was frequently found to be associated with chronic and severe marital disharmony which frequently included physical aggression, lack of financial support, infidelity and desertion by the spouse. The prevalence of this marital disharmony/depression cycle led the counselors to label it the "Pendeja Syndrome." Pendeja is a barrio Spanish term which means a fool or someone who submissively accepts abuse. A specific client who was said to have the Pendeja Syndrome was a woman who had endured many years of material neglect and infidelity as well as serious and frequent physical aggression by her alcoholic husband. She left him only after she saw him sharpening a long knife as he repeated loudly "It's not going to hurt. It's not going to hurt." At times, reported marital disharmony was very bizarre. For example, a woman stated that she had been severely bitten all over her body by her alcoholic husband. This was supported by the existance of visible scars. Another described losing her three month fetus as a result of being beaten while pregnant. A third related that her husband was refusing to provide her and her children with food in an effort to force her return to Mexico. Her emaciated and depressed appearance seemed consistent with her reported starvation.

Problems discussed during counseling. A content analysis of the counselors' summary notes for each counseling session revealed that the subjects discussed many problem areas. Those most frequently emphasized, however, were concerned with disharmony with husband or lover and the subject's relationship with her children.

Referral source. After four months of active recruitment utilizing multiple methods, only 42 calls were made requesting counseling. Of these 42 only 36 kept their appointments. These subjects were asked who had referred them or how they had learned of the availability of the special counseling. No one method of recruitment seemed to be outstandingly effective even though referral by agencies, especially by Mental Health, was most frequently reported.

The need for employing aggressive, multiple recruitment efforts utilizing ethnic-appropriate sources such as Spanish language newspapers and radio stations as well as community leaders and agencies should be strongly emphasized. Even when in desperate need of counseling services, this population does not readily seek out psychological assistance. Perhaps the severity of the subjects' problems, their depression, their poverty, and their lack of psychological sophistication contribute to their hesitancy to seek needed counseling services. This difficulty could contribute to the chronicity of their problems and to the perpetuation of these problems with their large families.

Use of transportation and/or baby-sitting. Although transportation and baby-sitting were available for all the subjects, these services were infrequently used. A majority of subjects (72.2 percent) did not use the available transportation, primarily because most of them (66.7 percent) came from nearby neighborhoods in Oxnard. This finding is consistent with that of Lehmann (1970) who reported that even though transportation was available, the majority of the poor who sought help from a community mental health center came from residences within a four block radius of the center. Another interesting finding was that the majority of the subjects were very prompt in their arrival to the counseling sessions.

Even though the subjects characteristically reported very large families, utilization of the available baby-sitting services was also low (16.7 percent) and may be explained in terms of the subjects being able to leave their younger children in the care of their older children who were free to baby-sit since all counseling was conducted on Saturday.

Experimental hypotheses. The results of the study indicate
that the behavior rehearsal treatment procedures produced significant differences in terms of therapeutic outcomes as measured
by the GAS on only one of the five scales. No significant differences between the two treatment conditions were obtained on the
other four scales, however, the means were in the predicted
direction. Significant differences in treatment attendance was
also not found in subjects exposed to Behavior Rehearsal. The
mean number of counseling sessions attended by the subjects
assigned to Therapeutic Listening was 5.15 and 5.16 for Behavior
Rehearsal. The relationship between treatment attendance and
therapeutic outcomes was tested by correlational analysis of
post-assessment GAS scores and number of counseling sessions
attended. The r for all subjects, regardless of treatment, was
-.15, for Behavior Rehearsal it was .16 and -.24 for Therapeutic
Listening. Thus, treatment attendance was negatively correlated
to therapeutic outcomes for all subjects and for subjects exposed
to Therapeutic Listening. The correlation of treatment attendance
and Behavior Rehearsal was positive but not at a traditional
level of significance.

The prediction that the subjects would more frequently
prefer Spanish in counseling was tested by chi-square analysis.
The null hypothesis was relected at the .01 level of significance.

There are several aspects of the study which may have con-
tributed to the results. Among others, these include:

1. The small n may have attenuated the differences between
the two treatment groups.

2. The small number of subjects who attended all eight
counseling sessions (8) may also have prevented the detection of
significantly different treatment outcomes.

3. The counselor-treatment interaction which seemed to
indicate that one counselor was more effective in therapeutic
listening while another was more effective with Behavior Rehearsal
may have prevented the detection of significant differences
between the two treatment conditions.

4. The pre-and post-assessment with the Goal Attainment Scale may not have been sensitive enough to measure therapeutic outcomes. Multiple criteria for measuring improvement might have been more effective in testing the effectiveness of the two treatment conditions.

5. All subjects were given immediate information and referral for auxiliary services such as welfare assistance, medical care, and legal aid. The therapeutic effects of these variable are not known.

6. Five client specific problem areas might have been too numerous to provide enough treatment concentration to effect favorable outcomes. It should be noted that the client's problems were described as very serious, while treatment attendance tended to be quite brief (Mean = 5.15).

7. The procedures utilized to train the counselors in the treatment conditions may have not been effective because of their short duration.

8. Neither of two treatment models - Behavior Rehearsal and Therapeutic Listening - may be particularly effective for ameliorating the particular problems presented by this population. Cognitive techniques and direct economic and social assistance may need to be prerequisites for these types of therapeutic programs.

Implications For Further Research

This study's findings, drawn from both the research questions and experimental hypotheses, suggests several implications for further research:

1. The prevalence of severe marital disharmony reported by the subjects as well as the high rates of "broken homes" reported by the Mexican Americans in general (cf: Barrett, 1966; Moore with Cuellar, 1970; Grebler et al., 1970) suggests the need to test marital counseling approaches with this population.

2. The language variable and its relationship to therapeutic outcomes needs further study. The importance of providing

bilingual counselors was supported by the study.

3. Continued comparison and testing of behavior counseling techniques with this population needs to be considered. Their tendancy to attend very few counseling sessions prevent the use of more traditional long-term therapies. Their pervasive poverty as well as their reported subassertiveness suggests the need for self help procedures, assertive training, and other behavioral techniques.

4. Auxiliary services such as referral to welfare assistance and medical care needs to be tested in regard to their effectiveness in promoting favorable therapeutic outcomes.

5. The results of this study also suggests that further research is needed to determine more fully the relationship of exposure to Behavior Rehearsal and favorable treatment outcomes. Multiple criteria for measuring treatment effectiveness are recommended, as well as restriction of the client's problem-area to one main category such as marital disharmony. This restriction could facilitate concentration of treatment time which might influence more favorable therapeutic outcomes.

Conclusions

The results of this investigation indicated that the subjects studied were disadvantaged, as evidenced by: their attaining very low levels of educational, vocational and economic achievements; speaking English infrequently; reporting high rates of severe marital disharmony; and by demonstrating symptoms consistent with the clinical diagnosis of depression. The two treatment models selected for testing with this population were not consistently effective in promoting favorable therapeutic outcomes. Perhaps neither Behavior Rehearsal nor Therapeutic Listening are appropriate for the types of problem areas reported by low income Mexican American women. Other innovative counseling approaches may need to be developed first to provide direct intervention in the client's environmental circumstances and later to modify the client's behavior and that of her husband.

These approaches would recognize the importance of early detection and intervention to prevent the chronicity and perpetuation of maladaptive behaviors in the client and her family. It may well be that low socio-economic Mexican American women cannot profit from exposure to more abstract counseling procedures until their immediate economic and social crisis are attenuated. These approaches, however, may be appropriate after the immediate problems are resolved to a point that the clients can begin working on their own personal behaviors. The need for effective detection-recruitment methods to reach and retain individuals needing psychological assistance also should be recognized. The nature of the problems of the low income Mexican American women - especially depression aggravated by pervasive poverty and marital disharmony - may deter them from seeking needed counseling. Counseling, as indicated by this study, if it is to be used by this population, needs to be provided in the client's preferred language in a setting which is culturally familiar as well as centrally located to their residences.

Additional research in which multiple detection-recruitment methods are tested, relationships of the language variable to treatment outcomes are explored, and comparisons are made of several innovative counseling approaches utilizing multiple criteria for measuring treatment outcomes is necessary before any conclusive support can be gained for hypotheses regarding counseling the low socio-economic Mexican American women.

REFERENCES

Alisky, M. The reporter, February 9, 1967.

Bandura, A. Psychotherapy based upon modeling principles. In A.E. Bergin & S.L. Garfield (Eds.), Handbook of psychotherapy and behavior change. New York: John Wiley & Sons, 1971.

Barrett, D.N. Demographic characteristics. In J. Samora (Ed.), La Raza: Forgotten Americans. London: University of Notre Dame Press, 1966.

Bereiter, C. Some persisting dilemmas. In C. Harris (Ed.), Problems in meaning change. Madison, Wisconsin: University of Wisconsin Press, 1967.

Bergman, D.V. Counseling Method and client responses. Journal of Consulting Psychology, 1951, 15, 216-224.

Bernstein, B. Social Class, speech systems and psychoterapy. In F. Reissman, J. Cohen, & A. Pearl (Eds.), Mental Health of the poor. New York: The Free Press, 1964.

Bernstein, B. A socio-linguistic approach to socialization - with some reference to educability. In F. Williams (Ed.), Language and poverty. Chicago: Markham Publishing Co., 1970.

Bureau of Biostatistics. Some selected 1970 population characteristics for California counties. Sacramento: January 15, 1972.

California Department of Mental Hygiene. M.I. admissions - 1969-1970, race vs. county. Sacramento: Author, 1970.

Campbell, D. T., & Stanley, J.C. Experimental and quasi-experimental designs for research. Chicago: Rand McNally & Co., 1963.

Clark, K. Dark ghetto. New York: Harper & Row, 1964.

Clausen, J.A. Values, norms, and the health called mental. In S.B. Sells (Ed.), The definition and measurement of mental health. Washington, D.C.: Dept. of Health, Education & Welfare, 1968.

Clinard, M.B. Slums and community development. New York: The Free Press, 1970.

deCharms, R., & Rosenbaum, M.E. Status variables and matching behavior. *Journal of Personality*, 1960, 28, 292-502.

Gardner, E. Concept of mental disorder: The relationship to criteria for case definition and methods of case detection. In S.G. Sells (Ed.), *The definition and measurement of mental health*. Washington, D.C.: Dept. of Health, Education and Welfare, 1968.

Gelfand, D.M. The influence of self-esteem on rate of verbal conditioning and social matching behavior. *Journal of Abnormal and Social Psychology*, 1962, 65, 259-265.

Glazer, N. The process and problems of language maintenance; An integrative review. In J.A. Fishman, V.C. Nahirny, J.E. Hofman, and R.G. Hayden (Eds.), *Language loyalty in the United States*. London: Mouteu & Company, 1966.

Grebler, L., Moore, J.W. & Guzman, R. C. *The Mexican-American people*. New York: The Free Press, 1970.

Haugen, E. *Bilingualism in the Americas: A bibliography and research guide*. Alabama: American Dialect Society, 1956.

Hennepin County Mental Health Center. *Dictionary and index of goal attainment scaling*. Minneapolis: Aug. 1971.

Hennepin County Mental Health Center. *Intake procedures manual for program evaluation*. Minneapolis: Aug. 1971.

Hennepin County Mental Health Center. *Programmed instruction in goal attainment scaling*. Minneapolis: Aug. 1971.

Hays, W.L. *Statistics*. New York: Holt, Rinehart & Winston, 1963.

Hollingshead, A.B. & REdlich, F.C. *Social class and mental illness*. New York: John Wiley & Sons, 1958.

Humphrey, H.H., Health services of the poor: A portrait of failure. In R.E. Will & H.G. Vatter (Eds.), *Poverty in affluence*. New York: Harcourt, Brace & World, 1965.

Jackins, H. *The human side of human beings*. Seattle: Rational Island Publishers, 1965.

Jaco, G.E. Mental health of the Spanish American in Texas. In M. Opler (Ed.), *Culture and mental health*. New York: MacMillan Co., 1959.

Jakubczak, L.F. & Walters, R.H. Suggestibility as dependency behavior. *Journal of Abnormal and Social Psychology*, 1959, 59, 102-107.

Kanariff, V.T. & Lanzetta, J.T. Effects of task definition and probability of reinforcement upon the acquisition and extinction of imitative responses. Journal of Experimental Psychology, 1960, 60, 340-348.

Karno, M. The enigma of ethnicity in a psychiatric clinic. Archives of General Psychiatry, 1965, vol. 14.

Karno, M. & Edgerton, R.B. Perception of mental illness in a Mexican-American community. Archives of General Psychiatry, 1969, Vol. 20.

Karno, M. & Morales, A. A community mental health service for Mexican-Americans in a metropolis. Comprehensive Psychiatry. 1971, 2, Vol. 12.

Kiresuk, T. Components of goal attainment scaling for individuals. Minneapolis: Program Evaluation Project, 1970.

Kiresuk, T. & Sherman, R. Goal attainment scaling: A general method for evaluating comprehensive community mental health programs. Community Mental Health Journal, 1968, 6, Vol. 4.

Krebs, R. Using attendance as a means of evaluating community mental health programs. Community Mental Health Journal, 1971, 1, Vol. 7.

Krumboltz, J.D. & Thoresen, C.E. (Eds.) Behavioral counseling: Cases and techniques. New York: Holt, Rinehart & Winston, 1969.

Langer, T.S. & Michael, S.T. Life stress in mental health - the midtown Manhattan study. New York: The Free Press, 1968.

Lazarus, A.A. Behaviour rehearsal vs. non-directive therapy vs. advice in effecting behaviour change. Behaviour Research and Therapy, 1966, 4, 209-212.

Lehmann, S. Selected self-help: A study of clients of a community social psychiatry service. American Journal of Psychiatry, 1970, 10, Vol. 126.

Leighton, D.C., Hardind, J.S., Macklin, D., MacMillan, A.M. & Leighton, A.H. The character of danger: Psychiatric symptoms in selected communities. New York: Basic Books, 1962.

Madsen, W. The Mexican American of south Texas. New York: Holt, Rinehart & Winston, 1964.

McMahon, J.T. The working class psychiatric patient: A clinical view. In F. Riessman, J. Cohen & A. Pearl (Eds.), Mental health of the poor. New York: The Free Press, 1964.

Mechanic, D. Illness and cure. In J. Kosa, A. Antonovsky & I.K. Zola (Eds.), Poverty and health - A sociological analysis. Cambridge, Mass.: Harvard University Press, 1969.

Mittlebach, F. & Marshall, G. The burden of poverty. In Mexican-American study project, advance report No. 5. Los Angeles: University of California, 1966.

Moore, J. & Cuellar, A. Mexican Americans. Englewood Cliffs, New Jersey: Prentice Hall, 1970.

Morales, A. Mental and public health issues. El Grito, Winter, 1970.

Nelson, B. Paradigmatic encounters in life and treatment. In M. Nelson et al. (eds.), Roles and paradigms in psycho-therapy. New York: Gruen Stratton, 1968.

Opler, M.K. Culture and social psychiatry. New York: Atherton Press, 1967.

Overall, B. & Aronson, H. Expectations of psychotherapy in patients of lower socio-economic class. In F. Riessman, J. Cohen & A. Pearl (Eds.), Mental Health of the poor. New York: The Free Press, 1964.

Penalosa F. The changing Mexican-American in southern California. Sociology and Social Research, July 1967.

Penalosa, F. Toward an operational definition of the Mexican American. Aztlan, 1970, 1, Vol. 1.

Riessman, F. The new approach to the poor. In M. Greenblatt, P.E. Emery & B.C. Glueck (Eds.), Poverty and mental health. Washington D.C.: Psychiatric Research Report No. 21, 1967.

Riessman, F. & Goldfarb, J. Role playing and the poor. In R. Riessman, J. Cohen & A. Pearl (Eds.), Mental Health of the poor. New York: The Free Press, 1964.

Rogers, C.R. Counseling and psychotherapy. Boston: Houghton Mifflin, 1942.

Ross, D. Relationship between dependency, intentional learning, and incidental learning in pre-school children. Journal of Personality and Social Psychology, 1966, 4, 374-381.

Ruesch, J. Disturbed Communication. New York: Norton, 1957.

Ruesch, J. Therapeutic Communication. New York: Norton, 1960.

Sells, S.B. Symposium summary, evaluation and moderator's recom-
     mendations to the national center for health statistics.
     In S.B. Sells (Ed.), The definition and measurement of mental
     health. Washington D.C.: Dept. of Health, Education &
     Welfare, 1968.

Shaffer, J. Paradigmatic psychotherapy and the low income patient.
     In M. Nelson et al. (Eds.), Roles and paradigms in psycho-
     therapy. New York: Gruen Stratton, 1968.

Tharp, R.G., Meadow, A., Lennhoff, S.G., & Satterfield, D. Changes
     in marriage roles accompanying the acculturation of the
     Mexican American wife. Journal of Marriage and the Family,
     1968, 3, 404-412.

Torrey, E.F. Mental health service: How relevant for urban
     Mexican-Americans? Stanford M.D., 1970, 2, Vol. 9.

U.P.I. Santa Barbara News Press, March 1, 1971.

Urban, H.B., & Ford, D.H. Some historical and conceptual per-
     spectives on psychotherapy and behavior change. In A.E.
     Bergin & S.L. Garfield (Eds.), Handbook of psychotherapy
     and behavior change: An empirical analysis. New York:
     John Wiley & Sons, 1971.

Vledman, D. Fortran programming for behavioral science. New
     York: Holt, Rinehart & Winston, 1967.

Webster, H., & Bereiter, C. The reliability of changes measured
     by mental test scores. In C. Harris (Ed.), Problems in
     meaning change, Madison, Wisconsin: University of Wisconsin
     Press, 1967.

Will, R., & Vatter, H.G. (Eds.), Poverty in affluence. New York:
     Harcourt, Brace & World, 1965.

Winer, B.J. Statistical principles in experimental design. New
     York: McGraw Hill, 1971.

Wolpe, J. Psychotherapy by reciprocal inhibition. Stanford:
     Stanford University Press, 1958.

Wolpe, J. The practice of behavior therapy. New York: Pergamon
     Press, 1969.

RECRUITMENT LETTER
(English and Spanish)

Dear Madam:

Please allow me to inform you of an opportunity which may be of interest to you.

The Ford Foundation has awarded me a grant to provide counseling to women of Mexican descent who wish assistance with marital, family or personal problems. This service will be <u>confidential</u> and <u>absolutely free</u>.

I am a bilingual registered nurse prepared at the Master of Science level. I work at the Santa Barbara County Mental Health Department and at the University of California (Extension) of Santa Barbara. I am well prepared and very experienced, and hope to receive my doctorate in June, 1972 from the University of California.

We can only accept a limited number of applicants. So if you are 21 years or over, of Mexican descent, and wish assistance with marital, family or personal problems, please call Mr. Hector Alvarez (487-5511, Ext. 4292) between 8 A.M. and 5 P.M. Ask him for an appointment with me. I will courteously attend you in an office in Oxnard.

If you are accepted to participate in this program, you will be offered transportation and baby-sitting to attend the counseling sessions.

Let me repeat, this program is <u>absolutely free</u> but limited. So it is very important that you be <u>sincerely interested in</u> self improvement.

Sincerely,

Teresa Ramirez Boulette

Apreciable Señora:

Hágame el favor de darme su muy attenta atención. Quiero informarle de una oportunidad que quizás le sea de interés.

El "Ford Foundation" me ha concedido unos fondos con el fin de ofrecer servicios consejeros a mujeres mejicanas o mejico americanas que deseen ayuda con problemas matrimoniales, familiares o personales. Estos servicios serán absolutamente gratis y confidenciales.

Yo hablo inglés y español, soy enfermera registrada, y trabajo en el Departmento de Salud Mental de Santa Barbara y en la Universidad de California (Extention) en Santa Barbara. Tengo bastante preparacion y experiencia y espero recivir mi doctorado en Junio 1972.

Nada más podemos aceptar a un número limitado de aplicantes. Si Ud. tiene 21 anos o mas, y si Ud. es mexicana y desea ayuda con sus problemas, llame al Señor Hector Alvarez (487-551 Ext. 4292) a las 8 A.M.--5 P.M. Pidale una cita conmigo. Yo la atenderé en una oficina en Oxnard.

Si Ud. es aceptada para participar en este programa le ofreceremos transportación y el cuidado de sus niños menores. Le repito, estos servicios son gratis pero limitados.

Así es que es muy importante que Ud. tenga un sincero interés en su mejoramiento propio.

Sinceramente,

Teresa Ramirez Boulette

APPENDIX B

CONSENT TO ACT AS SUBJECT FOR RESEARCH AND INVESTIGATIONS

Subject's name:_____ Date_____

L. I hereby authorize _____

Name of person(s) who will perform procedure(s) or investigation(s) and/or such assistants as may be selected by him to perform the following procedure(s) and investigation(s): (describe in detail)

on_____ (subject)

2. The procedure(s) and investigation(s) listed in Paragraph 1

has (have) been explained to me by _____.
                                              (name)

3. I understand that the procedure(s) and investigation(s) described in Paragraph 1 involve the following possible risks and discomforts: (describe in detail)

and that the potential benefits of the investigation are as follows:

4. I understand that I may terminate my participation in the study at any time.

Subject's Signature _____

Witness _____

(If the subject is a minor, or otherwise unable to sign, complete the following):

Subject is a minor (age_____), or is unable to sign because

_____

_____

(Father) _____   (Guardian) _____

(Mother) _____   (Other person and relationship) _____

INSTRUCTIONS TO RECEIVER:

   1. Original signed copy retained in departmental files.

   2. One signed copy forwarded to the Research Office.

INITIAL QUESTIONNAIRE

Subject No.:_____ Name:_____

Address:_____ Phone:_____

Counseling Language Preference:_____

Q. 1. Language usage at Home:

    1. Spanish   3. English primarily
    2. Spanish primarily   4. English only

Q. 2. Height:

    1. 4' or less   5. 4'1" - 5'4"
    2. 4'1" - 4'4"   6. 5'5" - 5'8"
    3. 4'5" - 4'8"   7. 5'9" - 6'
    4. 4'9" - 5'

Q. 3. Weight:

    1. 80 lbs. or less   6. 161 - 180 lbs.
    2. 80 - 100 lbs.   7. 181 - 200 lbs.
    3. 110 - 120 lbs.   8. 201 - 220 lbs.
    4. 121 - 140 lbs.   9. 221 or over
    5. 141 - 160 lbs.

Q. 4. Health Opinion:

    1. Excellent   3. Fair
    2. Good   4. Poor

Q. 5. Health Problems:

    0. None reported   5. Disturbed sleep
    1. High B/P   6. Difficult breathing
    2. Fatigue   7. Heart pressure or pain
    3. Nervous stomach   8. Other symptoms
    4. Headache/or neck   9. Multiple problems
       pain

Q. 6. Age:

1.	21-25	5.	41-45	9.	61-65
2.	26-30	6.	46-50	10.	Over 65
3.	31-35	7.	51-55		
4.	36-40	8.	56-60		

Q. 7. Marital Status:

1. Married   4. Divorced
2. Separated   5. Never Married
3. Widow

Q. 8. Times Married: _____

Q. 9. Number of Children (living and dead): ____ living, _____ dead

Q. 10. Occupation:

1. Unskilled   5. Medium white collar
2. Semi-skilled   6. High white collar
3. Skilled   7. Housewife
4. Low white   8. No answer
   Collar

Q. 11. First Husband's Occupation:

1. Unskilled   5. Medium white collar
2. Semi-skilled   6. High white collar
3. Skilled   7. No answer
4. Low white collar 8. No first husband

Q. 12. Second Husband's Occupation:

1. Unskilled   5. Medium white collar
2. Semi-skilled   6. High white collar
3. Skilled   7. No answer
4. Low white collar 8. No second husband

Q. 13. Father's Occupation:

1. Sunkilled   5. Medium white collar
2. Semi-skilled   6. High white collar
3. Skilled   7. Unknown
4. Low white collar 8. No answer

Q. 14. Education:

    0. None   4. High School graduate
    1. Some elementary   5. Some college
    2. Elementary graduate6. College graduate
    3. Some high school   7. No answer

Q. 15. Educated:

    1. Mexico
    2. USA
    3. No place
    4. No answer

Q. 16. First Husband's Education:

    0. None   4. High School graduate
    1. Some elementary   5. Some college
    2. Elementary graduate6. College graduate
    3. Some high school   7. No answer

Q. 17. Second Husband's Education:

    0. None   4. High school graduate
    1. Some elementary   5. Some college
    2. Elementary graduate6. College graduate
    3. Some high school   7. No answer

Q. 18. Husband Educated:

    1. Mexico
    2. USA
    3. No place
    4. No answer

Q. 19. Father's Education:

    0. None   5. Some college
    1. Some elementary   6. College graduate
    2. Elementary graduate   7. Unknown
    3. Some high school   8. No answer
    4. High school graduate

Q. 20. Father Educated:

    1. Mexico
    2. USA
    3. No place
    4. No answer

Q. 21. Total Family Income:_____ per month
     22. Number of Dependents:_____
     23. Number of Dependents in Mexico: _____
     24. Annual Income per Person:_____

Q. 25. Birthplace:

     1. Mexico   2. USA   3. Unknown

Q. 26. First Husband's Birthplace:

     1. Mexico   4. No answer
     2. USA   5. No husband
     3. Unknown

Q. 27. Second Husband's Birthplace:

     1. Mexico   4. No answer
     2. USA   5. No husband
     3. Unknown

Q. 28. Parents' Birthplace:

     1. Mexico   2. USA   3. Unknown   4. No answer

Q. 29. Referral Source:

     1. Letter   2. Agency 3. Radio   4. Community person

Q. 30. Transportation need:

     1. Yes   2. No

Q. 31. Baby-sitting need:

     1. Yes   2. No

Q. 32. Prior Counseling:

     1. Yes   2. No

Q. 33. Additional Services Needed:_____

Q. 34. Complete Physical Exam:

     1. 0-1 year   2. 1-2 years   3. Over 2 years

Q. 35. Additional Comments:

Interviewer's Opinion on the Following Subject Characteristics:

Q. 36. Dress: Traditional to Modern

1 2 3 4 5 6 7 8 9

Q. 37. Makeup: Traditional (no make-up) to Modern

1 2 3 4 5 6 7 8 9

Q. 38. Hair: Traditional (braids, etc.) to Modern

1 2 3 4 5 6 7 8 9

Q. 39. Skin Color: Dark Brown to Fair

1 2 3 4 5 6 7 8 9

A SAMPLE SUMMARY OF THE SUBJECT'S PROBLEMS AT INTAKE*

Subject Number:_____   Counselor Assignment:_____

Language Preference:_____   Treatment Assignment:_____

Date of Intake: _____   Appointment for 1st Counseling
                                    Session:_____

This 48 year old, Mexican native, Spanish only, unemployed, separated (11 years ago - left her for another woman), mother of nine children (two died, seven are now in Mexico) looks very depressed. Her current situation is very difficult. She reports coming to the U.S.A. illegally to stay with friends so that she could work to support her large, impoverished, family in Mexico. Shortly after her arrival she became ill with ovarian cancer. After many legal problems she managed to get the extensive medical treatment which she needed (free). Currently she is penniless and living off of the charity of her friends. She feels very badly that her physical condition prevents her from "earning her keep." At times she does not eat because she does not feel she deserves to eat food that is not hers.

Problem:
1. Decision making - is very ambivalent about continuing with needed medical treatment. Is considering terminating medical care and returning to Mexico. Knows this could result in her death.

2. Depression - much weight loss--poor appetite and refusal to eat.

3. Depression - brooding thoughts of impending death even though her doctor says she will get well.

_____

*This summary was personally reviewed by the investigator with the assigned counselor prior to the subject's first counseling session.

4. Depression - disturbed sleep - goes to bed at 8 p.m. and does not sleep until 1 or 2 a.m. even though she takes sleeping medication.

5. Guilt - feels very guilty that she did not marry her husband by The Church. Feels her cancer is a punishment by God.

APPENDIX E

THE GOAL ATTAINMENT SCALE

The following discussions and illustrations are some of
the materials provided by Hennepin County, Minnesota Mental
Health Center. Other available materials are Intake Procedures
Manual for Program Evaluation, Dictionary and Index for Goal
Attainment and Programmed Instruction in Goal Attainment
Scaling.*

HOW DOES THE GOAL ATTAINMENT SCALING SYSTEM WORK, IN GENERAL?

There are many variations on the exact pattern of Goal Attainment
Scaling, other than that used by the Program Evaluation Project.

Some of these variations are mentioned in the Commentary on "The
Variety of Current GAS Applications." All of them rely on the
basic system described below.

1. The client (a client could be any person relying on the
    services of the professional involved) is encouraged
    either by himself or with the aid of a professional to
    present his concerns. Except in special cases, no effort
    should be made to delimit the range of his concerns.

2. These concerns should be examined, again either by a profes-
    sional or by the client himself, so that a set of major
    concerns is isolated. No limits should be placed on the
    number of major concerns selected, except that there should
    be at least a representative of all relevent concerns.
    (See the Commentary on "Whose Goals Are on the GAS?" for a
    discussion of the determination of relevance.)

3. Once the major concerns have been selected, each one should
    become the subject of a separate SCALE. The SCALING is a
    systematic arrangement of the possible outcomes in the ful-
    fillment of the GOAL.

---

*All these materials may be obtained from the Program Evaluation
Project, 501 Park Avenue South, Minneapolis, Minnesota 55415.

FOR WHAT TYPE OF EVALUATION IS G.A.S. DESIGNED?

In the Program Evaluation Project, the G.A.S. system was developed in order to compare the effectiveness of four major Treatment-modes used at the Hennepin County Mental Health Center. These four MODES are: Drug Therapy, Individual Therapy, Group Therapy and Day-Care Therapy, all of which combine to form the Adult Out-Patient PROGRAM. The Mental Health Center contains other PROGRAMS, such as the In-Patient or the Child PROGRAM. All the programs combine in an AGENCY or center.

1. In other words, the comparisons carried on by P.E.P. are all intra-PROGRAM. Provisions are not included in the P.E.P.-design for comparisons between similar programs of different agencies.

2. In the type of evaluation performed by P.E.P., the Follow-up raters are totally separate from the Mental Health Center staff, where the different TREATMENT MODES are being carried out. This arrangement is considered desirable to minimize bias in treatment MODE comparisons. There are four main points of activity in the evaluation design.

    a. The intake or other point at which the Goal Attainment Follow-up Guide (G.A.F.G.) is constructed.

    b. The random assignment (where ethically proper) to a Treatment-mode.

    c. The treatment of the client by the professional or professionals.

    d. The follow-up, in which the degree of GOAL ATTAINMENT is rated.

        The professional undertaking treatment should not be involved in either GAFG construction or follow-up.

3. It is suggested that when comparisons among similar programs in different agencies are undertaken, the variable of "different GAFG constructors" should be eliminated by a personnel exchange program. Intake and Follow-up workers must be exchanged among agencies. It would also be desirable, but not always necessary for patients in similar programs to be randomly assigned to the agencies under comparison.

4. Each SCALE theoretically represents a continuum of observable measures from the worst anticipated outcome to the best anticipated outcome. In the case of the grid-shaped "follow-up guide" used by PEP, five levels are assumed on each SCALE, although not every scale needs to be filled out during the SCALING procedures. The EXPECTED OUTCOME

112

is given a value of zero, with the best anticipated at +2 and the worst expected at -2.

5. At the end of the treatment-process (that is, the inter-action between client and therapist) the client's GOAL ATTAINMENT is reexamined. His degree of ATTAINMENT in comparison to each GOAL is recorded on the grid-shaped "follow up guide." Each level of ATTAINMENT on each SCALE earns a score between -2 and +2. (It is possible, of course, to have more than one follow-up so that a range of ATTAINMENT scores could be collected for each SCALE).

6. This process leads to a cluster of scores for each client. These scores indicate the degree of GOAL ATTAINMENT. A positive score shows better than expected ATTAINMENT for a major concern and vice versa. Through a statistical formula called the T-SCORE, the overall GOAL ATTAINMENT of the client or client-group can be indicated.

WHERE SHOULD THE CLIENT'S "LEVEL AT INTAKE" BE PLACED ON THE GOAL ATTAINMENT FOLLOW-UP GUIDE (G.A.F.G.)?

The "level at intake" can be at ANY LEVEL at all, from -2 to +2. In general, each client's "level at intake" need not be at the same level on the G.A.F.G. The level at intake does not need to appear at all.

SCALE 5: DRUG USE $(w_5 =)$	EXAMPLE 1: If a non-cooperative heroin addict were sent to a Mental Health Center by his probation officer, it might be found that his "level at intake" was "drug usage every other day."	SCALE 4: SLEEPLESSNESS $(w_4 =)$
Twice daily (-2)	If the intake interviewer saw no chance of getting cooperation from the patient, he might expect the patient to deteriorate. Thus, the "level at intake" might be put at +1 or +2, and the zero level might be "drug usage every day."	One hour of sleep per night LEVEL AT INTAKE (-2)
Daily (0)	EXAMPLE 2: If a young woman came into a Mental Health Center complaining about sleeplessness due to deep depression, it might be found that her "level at intake" was "unable to sleep more than one hour per night." She might reasonably believe that things could not be expected	Four to five hours of sleep per night (0)
Every other day LEVEL AT INTAKE (+1)	to be any worse and that she could not survive long with that little sleep. The intake interviewer might decide that the patient could reasonably be expected to do nothing but improve.	(+1)
(+2)	Thus, the "level at intake" might be put at -2, and the zero level could be "sleeping from four to five hours per night."	Eight hours of sleep per night (+2)

EXAMPLE #1   EXAMPLE #2

HOW IS THE GOAL ATTAINMENT FOLLOW-UP GUIDE
(G.A.F.G.) CONSTRUCTED?

A key aspect of the GOAL ATTAINMENT SCALING procedure is the preparation of the GAFG. The GAFG. will be frequently scored by
someone other than the person who constructed it, so that pre-
cise, unequivocal development of the GAFG is essential to accurate
evaluation. The "Ten Commandments" of GOAL ATTAINMENT can be
consulted for some vital elements of GAFG-construction. The
follow-up (see #3, below) may be set individually for each client.
The example below may illustrate the general process.

1.

	X	Y	Z
-2			
-1			
0			
+1			
+2			

Major concerns, or GOALS, of the client are
isolated and each concern to be used is placed
at the head of a scale, described in a brief
phrase or "Scale Heading."

In this case, an educational situation, the
client had three main concerns: X (grades),
Y (reading speed), and Z (number of times sent
to the principal's office by the teacher).
Since no other major concerns are selected,
the last two vertical columns are left blank.

2.

	X	Y	Z
-2			
-1			
0	C-	200	3
+1			
+2			

The professional (a counselor) interviews the
client (a "problem-student") in order to help
construct the G.A.F.G. The client has an
average grade (Major Concern X) of D, a reading
speed of 50 words per minute (Major Concern Y),
and has been sent to the principal at least
6 times a month (Major Concern Z). Together
they estimate that the client could expect,
by the end of the school year (seven months),
to raise his average to C-, raise his reading-
speed to 200 words per minute, and lower his
visits to the principal to 3 per month, if
the client will cooperate in a counseling
and remedial reading program. These predic-
tions become zero levels for their respective
major concerns.

3.   Some of the other levels of the GAFG are then filled in. Not all levels need be filled, but the GAFG should be adequate for the follow up 7 months later, and must have at least 2 levels per scale.

    a. On Scale X (grades), the worse the client expects is that his average will fall to "F" (which is then put at -2) and the best he is likely to accomplish is "B+" (which then becomes +2).

    b. For Scale Y, the present reading speed is thought to be bad enough so that it is placed at -2 (50), and 400 words per minute is judged to be better than expected and placed at +1.

    c. For Scale Z, the current rate of 6 visits to the principal per month is placed at -1, and the best anticipated result is no visits to the principal, so zero is placed at +2.

4.   Finally, the scores are adjusted so that there are no gaps between the prediction-scores of the filled-in levels. The final GAFG will read like this and can be "followed-up" in 7 months.

	X	Y	Z			X	Y	Z
-2	F	50			-2	F	50	
-1			6		-1			6-4
0	C-	200	3		0	C-	200-	3
+1		400					400	
+2	B+		0		+1		400+	
					+2	B+		0

WHOSE GOALS ARE ON THE G.A.S.?

Many experimenters have relied on scales of "clinical rating"
or "therapist judgments" or something similar as a method of
determining how well a client has done in treatment. G.A.S. is
not such a device.

One of the unique features of the G.A.S. is that there is no
predetermined prejudice in favor of therapist-selected goals.
Either the patient or the therapist may choose the goals to
be examined. It is quite possible to use the G.A.S. either to
solicit directly the patient's goals for himself or to have a
compromise guide filled out with a combination of therapist
and patient goals. Patients in a group could determine goals
for each other or members of a family could join together to
form a collective G.A.S. guide.

Currently, P.E.P. is assisting in a substudy in which the goals
of the patient and therapist will be formally compared through
the use of G.A.S. guides (G.A.F.G.). The effect of goal-con-
currence and goal-dissonance on treatment-outcome will be analyzed
on a pilot-study basis.

In this era of increasing sensitivity to the existential uni-
queness of each patient, the Project hopes to provide a
foundation for avoiding the therapist bias present in many other
testing systems. It should prove possible, through G.A.S., to
incorporate the judgments and desires of the client into the
psychotherapy process, if agencies using G.A.S. wish to do so.

WHAT DOES A T-SCORE MEAN?

A T-Score is a statistical device designed to transform the weighted sum of the raw scores on the Goal Attainment Follow-up Guide (G.A.F.G.), (scores which range from -2 to +2) into a distribution where the mean is 50 (not zero, as on the GAFG raw scores) and the standard deviation is 10. The T-Score depends on the standard deviation for its units, and as a result neither it nor its raw-score equivalent can be calculated merely as an average of the raw score.

1. Any single T-Score can be translated into a position on the normal-curve (bell curve), and this normal-curve position can be used to derive a "percentile rank" revealing what proportion of the T-Score distribution is below the T-Score being analyzed. The T-Score to Percentile Rank Conversion Table can be consulted for such purposes.

2. A mean T-Score can be calculated for each different treatment mode within an agency's overall program and used to compare the treatment-modes or for other statistical analyses. The primary explanation of such a mean would be the severity of the Guides imposed on the agency by itself.

3. The mean T-Score for an entire agency has only minimal meaning. Such total agency means should not be used to compare the total care-effectiveness of two or more agencies unless the agencies collect only T-Scores constructed and followed-up by professionals who serve both agencies.

HOW IS THE T-SCORE CALCULATED?

This commentary explains the mechanics of calculating the T-SCORE, which is the final results of the GAS testing system. For the purposes of demonstration, the following sample GAS guide will be used:

	Scale 1 Happiness (w_1=10)	Scale 2 Creativity (w_2=5)	Scale 3 Accuracy (w_3=20)
-2			
-1		*	
0	*		
+1			
+2			*

On the GAS, 'w' stands for 'weight'. Thus, this GAS guide shows that the intake interviewer thought that 'Happiness' should be weighted 10, twice as important as the "Creativity" scale, which was only weighted 5.

The '*' shows the 'outcome level' of the client as scored by the follow-up rater. In other words, the client was scored at 0 on Scale 1, at -1 on Scale 2, and at +2 on Scale 3. On a real GAS guide, of course, each Scale would contain items pertaining to one of the areas of major concern for the client. THE WEIGHTS AND RAW SCORES ON THE GAS GUIDE ARE THE ONLY NUMBERS NEEDED TO CALCULATE THE T-SCORE. In the formula below, 'x' refers to the 'raw score' or 'outcome level'.

The formula for calculation is:

$$\text{T-SCORE} = 50 + \frac{10 \xi w_i x_i}{\sqrt{.7 \xi w_i^2 + .3(\xi w_i)^2}}$$

or 50 + 10(w_1 times x_1 + w_2 times x_2 + ...out to as many items as you have scales for)

$\sqrt{.7(w_1 \text{ squared} + w_2 \text{ squared} + ... \text{ out to as many items as you have scales for})}$ + .3 (all the weights added together)^2

The formula for this sample would read:

$$\text{T-SCORE} = 50 + \frac{10(w_1 x_1 + w_2 x_2 + w_3 x_3)}{\sqrt{.7 \left\{ (w_1)^2 = (w_2)^2 + (w_3)^2 \right\} + .3(w_1 + w_2 + w_3)^2}}$$

****

119

Using the Weights and Raw Scores from the demonstration guide above:

$$\text{T-SCORE} - 50 + \frac{10\left\{(0 \text{ times } 10) + (-1 \text{ times } 5) + (2 \text{ times } 20)\right\}}{\sqrt{.7\left\{(10)^2 + (5)^2 + (20)^2\right\} \stackrel{+}{-} .3(10 + 5 \_20)^2}} =$$

$$50 + \frac{10(0 - 5 + 40)}{\sqrt{.7(100 + 25 + 400) + .3(35)^2}} = 50 + \frac{10(35)}{\sqrt{.7(525) + .3(1225)}} =$$

$$50 + \frac{350}{\sqrt{367.5 + 367.5}} = 50 = \frac{350}{\sqrt{735}} = 50 + \frac{350}{27.11} = 50 + 12.91 = 62.91$$

HOW CAN THE T-SCORE BE CONVERTED TO A PERCENTILE RANK?

CONVERSION TABLE

This conversion is based on the fact that the T-Score is designed to have a normal distribution with a mean of 50 and a standard deviation of 10. The percentile rank of a particular T-Score shows the percentage of the distribution lying below that score.

T-SCORE	Theoretical Percentage Rank	T-SCORE	Theoretical Percentage Rank	T-SCORE	Theoretical Percentage Rank
21	less than .1	41	18	61	86
22	.1	42	21	62	88
23	.2	43	24	63	90
24	.3	44	27	64	92
25	.4	45	32	65	93
26	.6	46	34	66	94.5
27	.8	47	38	67	95.5
28	1.10	48	42	68	96.4
29	1.5	49	46	69	97.1
30	2.7	50	50	70	97.7
31	3.0	51	54	71	98.2
32	3.4	52	58	72	98.6
33	4	53	62	73	98.9
34	5	54	66	74	99.2
35	7	55	70	75	99.4
36	8	56	73	76	99.5
37	10	57	76	77	99.7
38	12	58	79	78	99.8
39	14	59	82	79	99.8
40	16	60	84	80	99.9
					99.9+

THE TEN COMMANDMENTS OF GOAL ATTAINMENT SCALING

1. Thou shalt not have less than two Scales on a guide.

2. Thou shalt not have less than two levels filled in for each Scale

3. Thou shalt have no false goals before thee, therefore, thou shalt not have more than one problem on each Scale.

4. Thou shalt not fill out they GAS guide in terms or abbreviations and catch-phrases, which thy follow-up scorer wilt not understand, either shalt thou scribble.

5. Know thou that thy client's behavior at intake may be at any of the five levels, or may be nowhere seen on thy GAS guide. Therefore, muzzle not thy client or thy patient by always putting behavior at intake nigh onto the 0 or -1 level.

6. Thou shalt not make goals which are too general to be useful.

7. Thou shalt not make goals which can not be told apart, one level from another, neither shalt thou make goals which can not possibly be measured.

8. Honor thy follow-up scorer, remember thee well that the follow-up must be brought about by him and should be data thou art sure he can locate in a follow-up interview.

9. Remember thy whole Scale and keep it whole; there should be no 0 levels which are so high that there is no possible +2 level. Similarly, therefore, with 0 goals which are so low that there is no possible -2 level.

10. Thou shalt have no other Scales which go higher than +2 nor lower than -2.

WHY IS THE G.A.S. SO UNIQUE?

It is unlikely that you have used a testing system very much like G.A.S. So far as study of the research literature has revealed, there is no other test really similar to the Goal Attainment Scaling system. Goal Attainment Scaling has special advantages which could prove useful in appropriate programs.

1. CLIENT-SPECIFIC

   In proper GAS use, there is no set number of goals and no pre-determined subjects to be included as goals. Whatever concerns seems appropriate to the needs of the client, whether the client is a program, a clinic, a patient, or a study, may be incorporated into a GAS guide.

2. GUIDE CONSTRUCTION

   GAS guides have been constructed by a wide range of persons: clinical psychologists, social workers, psychiatrists, administrators, psychiatric nurses, and clients themselves. Generally, between one and three hours of group instruction are required to develop skill in constructing GAS guides. Alternately, a follow up guide (GAFG) may be constructed with the assistance of someone already skilled in GAS usage. The professional, the client by himself, or the client and the professional together can build the GAFG. Even families, relatives or other involved parties could be guide-constructors.

3. GOAL-SETTING PRACTICE

   As an education device or a part of therapy interaction, even overlooking the measurement functions, the GAS system is very useful. If carefully applied, it could orient clinical, administrative or educational personnel to the advantages of systematic, consistent, goal-setting. Objectives and priorities for therapy or other inter-actions may be clarified if GAS is used as a goal-formulating tool.

GOAL ATTAINMENT FOLLOW-UP GUIDE

Scale Headings and Scale Weights

SCALE ATTAINMENT LEVELS	SCALE 1: $(w_1 =)$	SCALE 2: $(w_2 =)$	SCALE 3: $(w_3 =)$	SCALE 4: $(w_4 =)$	SCALE 5: $(w_5 =)$
a) Most unfavorable treatment outcome thought likely (-2)					
b) Less than expected success with treatment (-1)					
c) Expected level of treatment success (0)					
d) More than expected success with treatment (+1)					
e) Most favorable treatment outcome thought likely (+2)					

PROGRAM USING G.A.S. _____

TREATMENT RELIABILITY

Rater's Name _____
Tape Number _____

Directors: Please listen to each tape carefully and then record the counselor's performance which, in your opinion, is most frequently demonstrated. Be sure to select either a or b for each category even in those instances in which neither response appears appropriate. No discussion is permitted.

I. Counselor/Client Verbalizations

____ a Counselor primarily listens to the client and seldom attempts to control the quantity and/or the type of client verbalization.

____ b Counselor talks as needed; uses some leading and non-leading responses as well as listening behavior.

II. Type of Counselor Verbal Responses

____ a Counselor uses directive as well as some non-directive responses, e.g., tells the subject specifically what she needs to learn or do. Uses leading phrases such as "Let's get back to ..." "I want you to ..." "You need to ..." etc. Uses some non-leading responses such as "Hmmm hmmm." "I see ..." "And then?"

____ b Counselor uses few, if any, directive responses. The majority of her responses are non-directive such as "Yes?" "And then?" "Hmmm hmmm." etc.

III. Counselor Techniques

A.

____ a The counselor primarily uses reflection, paraphrasing and summarization verbal techniques, e.g., "Yes?" "You have been talking about her anger with your husband and ..."

____ b The counselor primarily uses action techniques, e.g., role playing, demonstration, imitation, and/or practice of a behavior to help the subject with her problems.

B.

_____ a The counselor encourages the client to
practice behaviors in and out of the
counseling session, e.g., her work and/or
home situation.

_____ b The counselor does not encourage the subject to engage in any specific behaviors
at home or at work. The focus is primarily
on helping the client gain insight and/or
emotional release within the session itself.

IV. In general, after listening to the counseling session I would
say that it best fits a

_____ Therapeutic Listening counseling session.

_____ Behavior Rehearsal counseling session.

Rater Selection and Training. The two tape raters were selected
according to the following criteria:

1. Verbal fluency in English and Spanish.

2. Experience with the culture of the poor and of the
Mexican American.

3. First year training in a two year program in a counseling psychology graduate program.

The raters were given two hours of instruction by the
investigator. The two treatment conditions - Behavior Rehearsal
and Therapeutic Listening were discussed in a similar manner
as with the counselors. Counselor responses specific to each
treatment model which have been described in Treatment Conditions
in Chapter II, were discussed and demonstrated. Additionally,
ten minute sections of six tapes, one for each treatment condition and each counselor, were played to provide rating practice
for the two raters. Rater reliability was established.

After the two hours of instruction, two tapes were randomly
selected for each counselor and each treatment conditions. The
first thirty minutes of each tape were played. The raters were
instructed not to talk or in any way discuss their ratings.
After listening to each tape the raters were instructed to inde-
pendently identify the counselor responses by using the rating
scale. After all of the tapes were rated, interjudge reliability
was established for each of the five sections of the Rating Scale
(r_1 = .66, 4_2 = .85, r_3 = 1, r_4 = 1, r_5 = 1).

APPENDIX G

PROBLEM AREAS OF SCALE II (GAS) ON WHICH SIGNIFICANT IMPROVEMENTS WERE GAINED BY SUBJECTS EXPOSED TO BEHAVIOR REHEARSAL

Problem Area	Frequency	Rank
Symptoms of depression	10	1
Disharmony with husband or lover	4	2
Social withdrawal	3	3
Inability to verbalize anger and/or sorrow	3	4
Disharmony with children	2	5
Anxiety symptoms	2	6
Sexual problems	2	7
Low motivation to attend counseling	1	8